GROUNDLESS BELIEF
An Essay on the Possibility of Epistemology

GROUNDLESS BELIEF

An Essay on the Possibility of Epistemology

Second Edition

MICHAEL WILLIAMS

PRINCETON UNIVERSITY PRESS
PRINCETON, NEW JERSEY

Library of Congress Cataloging-in-Publication Data

Williams, Michael, 1947 July 6–
    Groundless belief : an essay on the possibility of epistemology :
with a new preface and afterword / Michael Williams.
        p.   cm.
    Includes bibliographical references and index.
    ISBN 0-691-00907-4 (pbk. : alk. paper)
    1. Knowledge, Theory of.   I. Title.
BD161.W47   1999
121—dc21   99–17411

The paper used in this publication meets the minimum requirements of
ANSI/NISO Z39.48-1992 (R1997) (*Permanence of Paper*)

http://pup.princeton.edu

Printed in the United States of America

1   3   5   7   9   10   8   6   4   2

Contents

For my mother

Acknowledgments

This book is a revised version of the doctoral thesis I wrote at Princeton in 1973. I wish to thank numerous friends and teachers at Princeton, and particularly Gilbert Harman, for all the help I received. Special words of thanks are due to Meredith Swenson for being an unfailing source of advice and encouragement, to Michael Woods, my former tutor at Oxford, who encouraged me to revise the manuscript for publication, and to an anonymous reviewer whose many helpful suggestions assisted me in the process of revision. Also, I must not forget to mention two other former teachers: John Foster, under whose guidance I first began to think seriously about the topics discussed in this book, and A. J. Ayer, whose influence will be obvious to anyone who reads it.

Of the philosophers who have influenced me through their writings, those who have influenced me most are W. V. Quine and Wilfrid Sellars. A reviewer pointed out to me that some of the views I defend have been advocated on various occasions by Popper. To my regret, I had not read Popper before the manuscript was complete and so was not influenced directly, though I now agree that Popper is a philosopher whose epistemological views deserve serious attention.

Finally, my greatest debt of all is to Richard Rorty from whom I have learned more than from any other single person, and without whose ever-present support this book would never have been written.

New Haven, Connecticut
December, 1975

If there be no datum given to the mind, then knowledge must be contentless and arbitrary; there would be nothing which it must be true to.

C. I. Lewis, *Mind and the World Order*

So in the end when one is doing philosophy one gets to the point where one would like just to emit an inarticulate sound.

Wittgenstein, *Philosophical Investigations* 261.

Preface to the Second Edition

Looking back on *Groundless Belief,* I find various points to clarify but little that I would simply repudiate. On the whole, or so I like to think, the main line of argument wears fairly well. Certainly, some conclusions are over-stated. In particular, my remarks on the death of epistemology now strike me as too simple, though (charitably construed) not altogether wrong. I take up this and other points in a brief Afterword. Otherwise, I have let the argument stand.

Michael Williams
Evanston, Illinois
November 1998

1. Introduction: Epistemology and Scepticism

1. INTRODUCTORY REMARKS

In this essay I shall be concerned with the philosophical problem of perceptual knowledge and, especially, with an approach to that problem which I shall call 'phenomenalism'. I understand that term in a broad sense to be explained and defended as my argument proceeds. My interest in the topic is both philosophical and metaphilosophical: philosophical in that I shall argue that any theory of perceptual knowledge which is phenomenalistic in my sense is radically defective; and metaphilosophical in that I want to use my discussion of phenomenalism to raise, in a fairly concrete form, the question of whether epistemology, as traditionally conceived, constitutes a coherent intellectual discipline. I shall argue that it does not.

Many contemporary philosophers would agree that epistemological theories are best seen as offering different ways of reacting to the threat of scepticism. I think that this view is appealing on both philosophical and historical grounds.[1] But I also think that it is not the whole story.

It is sometimes said that associating epistemology too

---

[1] For an examination of the historical importance of scepticism and its relationship to modern epistemology, see R. H. Popkin, 'The Sceptical Origins of the Modern Problem of Knowledge', in Norman S. Care and Robert H. Grimm (eds.), *Perception and Personal Identity* (Cleveland, Ohio: Case Western Reserve University Press, 1969).

closely with scepticism gives a distorted picture of the subject. For example, a recent writer claims that the task of the epistemologist is not to refute scepticism but to show, given that knowledge is possible, how it is possible.[2] However, this strikes me as a distinction without a difference and, in any case, the claim rests on a misunderstanding of the view that epistemological theories are concerned with responding to scepticism. This view need not be taken to imply that there are sceptics who need to be refuted or that we have doubts, say about the reality of the external world, which need to be allayed. Rather, the point is that there are certain seemingly plausible arguments which purport to show that scepticism is true, and that different epistemological theories can be seen as different ways of meeting such arguments. That is to say, epistemological theories can be seen as the result of assuming that the conclusions of sceptical arguments are false and arguing, on this basis, either that the arguments are invalid or that they contain false premises. Such a strategy, it seems to me, amounts to an attempt to show that knowledge is possible, given that it is possible. More than this, if sceptical arguments did not exist, I do not think that any content could be given to the idea of showing that knowledge is possible. The task is a meaningful one just because there exist arguments purporting to show that knowledge is impossible. And indeed, this same writer admits that traditional theories of perceptual knowledge can be seen as arising out of objections to various steps in a certain pattern of sceptical argument. Such a connection can hardly be accidental.

Similar remarks apply to Chisholm's attempt to divorce the epistemological enterprise from sceptical doubts.[3]

[2] John Pollock, 'What is an Epistemological Problem', *American Philosopical Quarterly* (1968), pp. 183-190.

[3] A clear statement of Chisholm's metaphilosophical views is to be found in his contribution to *Humanistic Scholarship in America, The Princeton Studies: Philosophy* (Englewood Cliffs, N.J.: Prentice-Hall, 1964.

Chisholm thinks that an epistemological theory should be a contribution to an analytic science of evidence. An acceptable theory will recognize a certain order of epistemological priority amongst our beliefs and will lay down principles of evidence in virtue of which more primitive beliefs can be said to justify or confer reasonableness upon less primitive beliefs.

But what is the point of this analytic science? 'Analysing' concepts is not, I take it, something which is done simply for its own sake. Neither can Chisholm's approach to questions of justification be seen as a contribution to the sociology of knowledge: that is, he is not just interested in what people actually say when asked to justify their beliefs. Such an investigation would not reveal the kind of epistemological order he professes to find. People do not, in general, go in for systematic attempts to justify their beliefs at large. Certainly, they are not to be found offering ultimate justifications by appealing to classes of epistemologically primitive truths.

What Chisholm is looking for is the 'logical' structure of justification. This structure is uncovered by asking questions about justification in a highly systematic way. That is, Chisholm raises the questions one would raise *if* one were entertaining sceptical doubts about human knowledge. Using scepticism this way as a methodological device does not imply that any actual doubts are being entertained, so I do not think that it does any real violence to Chisholm's approach to epistemology to see it as involving a kind of methodological scepticism. In fact, it makes his position more intelligible. I shall have more to say about Chisholm's programme as my argument progresses.

2. RADICAL SCEPTICISM

I have said that epistemological theories can be seen as

offering different ways of reacting to the threat of scepticism, but I have a particular kind of scepticism in mind which I shall call 'radical scepticism'.[4]

By 'radical scepticism' I mean the thesis that one is never justified in believing anything at all. But we can also talk about radical scepticism about such and such—say, other minds, or the external world. Then we have more limited theses to the effect that one is never justified in believing anything about the minds of others or the external world or whatever.

I appeal to the notion of radical scepticism because it is the most interesting form of scepticism and the most important philosophically. Its interest and importance derive from its being formulated in terms of justified belief. I want to distinguish this interesting form of scepticism from forms of scepticism which amount to little more than carping about the use of the verb 'to know'. For example, it has been thought that knowing precludes even the logical possibility of error. Since little or nothing meets this strong condition, it is concluded that we believe much but know little or nothing. Hume in the *Treatise* wanted to distinguish three kinds of justified belief which he called 'knowledge, proofs and probabilities':

> By knowledge, I mean the assurance arising from the comparison of ideas. By proofs, those arguments which are derived from the relation of cause and effect, and which are entirely free from doubt and uncertainty. By probability, that evidence which is still attended with uncertainty.[5]

Proofs do not yield knowledge because there is always the possibility, however remote, that what has been 'proven' should turn out to be false. Anyone inclined to accept

[4] Following Gilbert Harman, *Thought* (Princeton: Princeton University Press, 1973).

[5] Hume, *Treatise of Human Nature,* Bk. 1, Pt. III, Sect. XI.

Hume's usage would have to hold that we have no 'knowledge' of the external world, or of what is going on in the minds of other people (if such there are), and so on. But this kind of scepticism is not very interesting once we realize what is going on. We can allow philosophers of Hume's persuasion to use 'knowledge' in their idiosyncratic way and let that be the end of it. Of course, that isn't always the end of it with philosophers like Hume. But this is because, when we look into the motivation for the idiosyncratic use of 'knowledge', we find, in spite of all the talk about freedom from doubt and uncertainty, the idea that there is something intrinsically second-rate about the kind of justification we have for, say, our beliefs about the physical world; and this brings us back into the domain of what I called 'radical scepticism'. The 'scepticism' which results from narrowing the normal use of 'know' is interesting only as a symptom of a deeper problem.

3. KNOWLEDGE AND JUSTIFICATION

Some recent discussion in the theory of knowledge has centred around attempts to formulate necessary and sufficient conditions for its being true that S know that P. This problem was brought into prominence by Gettier in an influential paper which presented arguments to show that the traditional conditions for knowledge—justified true belief—were insufficient.[6]

Gettier's strategy was to construct examples in which a person makes what seems to be a warranted inference from a justified but false belief to a belief which happens to be true, though its truth has nothing to do with the premise from

---

[6] Edmund L. Gettier, 'Is Justified True Belief Knowledge?' *Analysis* 23 (1963), pp. 121-123. Gettier's article provoked an enormous amount of discussion. For an extensive bibliography see Michael D. Roth and Leon Galis, *Knowing* (New York: Random House, 1970).

which it was inferred. Linguistic intuitions, it is claimed, tell us that such cases do not count as cases of knowledge, though they do count as cases of justified true belief.

Gettier's original examples are of a fairly restrestricted kind. It is essential to such examples that the subject make an inference. But some writers use the phrase 'Gettier example' in a wider sense to apply to any example designed to show that the traditional conditions for knowledge are insufficient.[7] Consider the following case: it looks to a perceiver as if there is a candle in front of him. Further, suppose that there really is a candle in front of him, so that his belief is true, although the candle he actually sees is one placed off to the side reflected in a mirror. If he has no reason to suspect such an elaborate deception, he will be justified in believing that there is a candle in front of him. Again, we have a case of justified true belief which, intuitively, does not count as knowledge.

How does Gettier's problem—the problem of formulating necessary and sufficient conditions for knowledge—relate to the dominant concerns of traditional epistemology? On the face of things, only distantly. I am arguing that epistemological theories such as phenomenalism, direct realism and so on, can be seen as different ways of reacting to the threat of radical scepticism. The important point to bear in mind is that radically sceptical theses are stated in terms of justified belief: thus traditional epistemological theories attempt to tell us something about justification, but they do not necessarily pretend to offer analyses of knowledge, in the sense of answers to Gettier's problem.

There is, however, a possible source of confusion here. Scepticism is often taken to be the thesis that knowledge is impossible. Given the traditional analysis of knowledge in terms of justified true belief, this amounts to radical scepticism. But if we take the traditional conditions to be insuf-

[7] E.g. Harman, op. cit.

ficient, we have to recognize two ways in which the possibility of knowledge might be denied. The first of these is radical scepticism which denies the possibility of justified belief, a necessary condition for knowledge. But a second, and to my mind much less interesting, form of scepticism can result from adding to the justified true belief condition, in an attempt to reach conditions which are sufficient as well as necessary, a further condition which turns out to be rarely, if ever, satisfied. The position thus reached, especially if stated in terms of the impossibility of knowledge, can look like radical scepticism. However, failure to *know* anything, now that knowledge is no longer equated with justified true belief, is compatible with being justified in believing all sorts of things and so does not amount to being landed in the position of the radical sceptic.

An example of a kind of scepticism which falls short of radical scepticism has been defended by Peter Unger.[8] His argument takes off from a distinction between 'absolute' and 'relative' terms. These are distinguished by a paraphrastic test. If we take an absolute term like 'flat', a sentence like 'My table is flatter than yours' can be paraphrased by 'My table is more nearly flat than yours.' But if we consider a relative term like 'bumpy', such a paraphrase will not work. The sentence 'My table is bumpier than yours' does not mean the same as the sentence 'My table is more nearly bumpy than yours.' This latter sentence does not even make much sense.

We can obtain similar results for some epistemic terms. (I do not follow Unger's own examples exactly.) Thus, 'John's claim is more certain than Bill's' can be rendered as 'John's claim is more nearly certain than Bill's', whereas 'John's claim is more confident than Bill's' cannot be rendered as 'John's claim is more nearly confident than Bill's.' By the

---

[8] In 'A Defence of Scepticism', *Philosophical Review*, LXXX, number 2 (April 1971), pp. 198-211.

paraphrastic test, 'certain' is an absolute term while 'confident' is not.

Unger argues that absolute terms are only dubiously applicable. In the case of an absolute term, F, it is rarely, if ever, the case that anything is, strictly speaking, (absolutely) F. Is anything we encounter absolutely flat? If we look more closely, say through a microscope, we find bumps. More importantly, is anything we believe ever absolutely certain? Surely not, for there is always the possibility that we have made some kind of mistake. Evidence of human fallibility is all too common.

Does knowing require being absolutely certain? That it does is shown, according to Unger, by the fact that it is linguistically anomalous to say things like 'I know it's raining but I'm not absolutely certain.' The sense of anomaly can be heightened by putting in suitable emphases to show that the claim to knowledge is to be taken literally. Thus consider the sentence 'He *really* knows, but he isn't certain.' Unger claims that this is a contradiction, and so knowing must entail being certain. Since 'certain' is an absolute term, and since absolute terms, taken strictly, are rarely, if ever, applicable, it follows that there is hardly anything, if anything at all, that any of us really knows.

This conclusion strikes me as remarkably uninteresting. That Unger's scepticism is not radical scepticism is shown by the fact that he is quite prepared to admit that 'there is much that many of us correctly and reasonably believe'.[9] But he thinks that much more is required for us to *know* anything at all. This 'more' turns out to be certainty, so the 'scepticism' which has been defended amounts to no more than the claim that little or nothing is absolutely certain. It is conceded that much of what we believe may be highly, even overwhelmingly, probable, so there is a clear sense in which it matters not at all whether this kind of scepticism is true or

[9] Unger, op. cit., p. 198.

false. The thesis is made to look more interesting than it really is by calling it 'a defence of scepticism'. The term 'scepticism' suggests radical scepticism, a thesis which threatens, if true, to undermine all of our commonsensical beliefs, and which therefore deserves to be taken seriously. The kind of scepticism which Unger argues for has no such implications.

Actually, Unger's argument is weak even in its own terms. The weakest link is the inference from the alleged oddity of sentences like 'He knows it's raining but he isn't certain' to the conclusion that knowing entails being certain, in Unger's strong sense of the word. The inference depends on the principle that the best way to explain why such sentences strike us·as anomalous is to suppose that they contain an implicit contradiction. But this principle is not generally valid. Suppose that I say 'It's raining but I don't believe it.' This would be a queer thing to say. If I assert something, in normal circumstances, I give the impression that I believe it, which is one reason for its being odd to go on to cancel the inference which my audience would normally make. But it could hardly be said that my utterance contains a contradiction. The fact that it is raining is quite compatible with my not believing that it is.

The purpose of this discussion has been to sharpen the notion of radical scepticism and to make clear how it differs from other positions which have been thought to be sceptical. Also, I wanted to clarify the claim that epistemological theories can be seen as different ways of reacting to the threat of radical scepticism. It turns out that traditional epistemological theories such as phenomenalism and direct realism (which aim to show how it is possible for us to have justified beliefs about the physical world), logical behaviorism (which attempts to do the same for our beliefs about the mental states of other people), operationalism with respect to the entities postulated by theoretical science, and so on, are candidates for being so regarded. Epistemological theories concerned with the 'analysis of knowledge'—where giving an analysis of knowledge is understood to be offering a solution to Gettier's problem—have no obvious connexion with radical scepticism. It would also seem to follow that such theories have no obvious connexion with the dominant concerns of epistemology, as that subject has been generally understood.[10] Traditional epistemology is concerned with the nature of justification, not with stating necessary and sufficient reasons for the truth of 'S knows that P'.

Since my concern in this essay is with certain traditional epistemological theories—those that I think of as, in a broad sense, phenomenalistic—I shall not venture a solution to the Gettier problem. However, my reason for this is not simply a matter of a different focus of interest. The history of the various attempts to formulate necessary and sufficient conditions for knowledge suggests that, although we may share reliable linguistic intuitions about which cases are to count as cases of knowledge, there may be no way to codify these intuitions in the form of a definition, any more than there is a way to codify our intuitions about what activities count as games. I do not find this an especially disturbing position to be in.[11]

I have been assuming so far that knowledge is to be under-

---

[10] An exception might be Plato's *Theaetetus*.

[11] Just how reliable our intuitions are in some recent problem cases is a matter for dispute. Harman (op. cit., p. 143) proposes the following case:- A political leader is assassinated. To forestall a coup, his associates pretend that the bullet hit someone else and announce on nationwide television that the would-be assassin's bullet struck a secret service man. However, a reporter gets the real story to his paper which includes the story in its final edition. Jill buys a copy and reads the true story. Harman claims that the widely disseminated counter-evidence undermines Jill's *knowing* that the leader has been assassinated. But suppose that a saboteur had cut the wire leading to the television transmitter just as the leader's associates were about to make their announcement: In this case, Jill would come to know that the leader had been assassinated. The only people who would have heard the announcement would have been those in the studio, all of whom were parties to the deception. '. . . a cut wire makes the

stood in terms of justification plus truth, even though I do not intend to formulate an additional requirement to account for our reluctance to count certain cases of justified true belief as cases of knowledge. But some writers have taken the existence of Gettier examples to show that the concept of justification is simply irrelevant to the analysis of knowledge.[12] Thus it is sometimes said that one has knowledge if the truth of one's belief is not accidental: that is, knowledge is true belief which is the outcome of a reliable process. This is a radical conclusion to draw from the insufficiency of the justified-true-belief analysis of knowledge but, if correct, doesn't it mean that the theories I want to discuss are simply irrelevant to the topic of perceptual knowledge?

I am inclined to reply that, if this were so, it would show that the concept of knowledge was devoid of epistemological interest. I should simply give up using the word 'knowledge' and, instead, conduct my discussion explicitly in terms of 'justification'. But such analyses do not show that the concept of justification is irrelevant to questions about knowledge. They show at most that we do not always expect people to whom we are inclined to ascribe knowledge actually to be in possession of the justification for their beliefs. That is, they show at most that we are prepared to countenance as cases of knowledge cases of *justifiable* true belief (belief reached by a *reliable* method—reasons for attaching credibility to such a belief could, in principle, be given).

difference between evidence that undermines knowledge and evidence that does not undermine knowledge' (Harman, op. cit. p. 147).

Not everyone has clear intuitions about cases like these. But even if everyone did, it would seem to me that such cases constitute a reductio ad absurdum of the idea that it is worthwhile to try to formulate conditions which account for linguistic intuitions about the use of the word 'know'.

[12] See e.g. Peter Unger, 'An Analysis of Factual Knowledge', *The Journal of Philosophy*, 65, 6 (March 21, 1968), reprinted in Roth and Galis.

Thus, in what follows, I shall continue to use the word 'knowledge' in a colloquial way, even though my main interest is in justification. My usage is not intended to prejudge any issues arising out of objections to the justified-true-belief analysis. I shall not offer a solution to Gettier's problem.

4. THE SCEPTICAL ARGUMENT

I remarked at the outset that there is a lot to be said for the view that traditional epistemological theories are best seen as offering different ways of reacting to the threat of radical scepticism. But how could radical scepticism ever come to be seen as a *threat*? Suppose we ask whether the physical world really exists, or whether there are really physical objects having any of the characteristics we normally take such things to have: G. E. Moore answers by holding up his hands in good light, as a result of which at least two such objects are known to exist.[13] Moore's demonstration is apt to strike us as slightly absurd: surely the sceptical question is meant to cut a little deeper than *that*. And indeed, it is often thought Moore's Johnsonian way with sceptical questions simply misses the point. But then what is the point?

Locke was prepared to confront the sceptic with more sophisticated empirical arguments. For example, he argued that some perceptions must be produced in us 'by exterior causes affecting our senses' because 'those that want the organs of any sense can never have the ideas belonging to that sense produced in their minds'.[14] Bennett, in his recent commentary, presents a typical reaction to Locke's argument. It is, he remarks, question-begging because it has

---

[13] G. E. Moore, 'Proof of an External World', *Proceedings of the British Academy*, Vol. XXV, 1939.

[14] Locke, *Essay*, IV.XI.4. Quoted by Jonathan Bennett in his *Locke, Berkeley, Hume: Central Themes* (Oxford: Clarendon Press, 1971), p. 66.

a premise about sense-organs, which are among the 'things without us' whose reality is in question.[15] Clearly, Moore's performance invites a similar comment.

Radical scepticism about the physical world says that we are never so much as justified in holding any of the beliefs we do about physical objects. We are not even justified in believing that there is an external world at all. But now it begins to look as if any attempted justification has to meet some fairly strict conditions. In particular, since all our beliefs about the physical world are up for validation at once, any 'justification', if it is not to be question-begging, must appeal to some quite distinct set of facts, knowledge of which does not presuppose knowledge of the physical world. Knowledge of such facts—often taken to be facts about the content of 'immediate experience'—is assumed to be required if we are to have any justification for the beliefs we hold about the physical world; but, in the last analysis, the reverse does not hold. Thus we reach the idea of a strict epistemological order. Our justification for holding beliefs of a certain kind must be traceable, ultimately, to a body of knowledge 'epistemologically prior' to such beliefs. Knowledge to which nothing is epistemologically prior may be called 'epistemologically basic' or 'foundational'. I shall call this view of justification—the view that there is a strict epistemological order—'the foundational view'.

Once we accept a foundational view of justification, and agree that there is a strict epistemological order, arguments for radically sceptical positions are not difficult to find. Ayer has shown that such arguments follow a common pattern.[16] Although I shall concentrate on the form of the argument most relevant to our perceptual knowledge of the physical world, this sceptical argument is easily generalizable and can

---

[15] Bennett, op. cit., p. 66.
[16] A. J. Ayer, *The Problem of Knowledge* (Pelican Books, 1956). See especially ch. 2, sect. ix.

be adapted to cast doubt on our right to hold beliefs about the mental life of other people, elementary particles, events in the past, and so on. The natural outcome of the argument, globally applied, is solipsism of the present moment (at the very least!).

According to Ayer, the argument calls in question a particular form of factual inference in which 'we appear to end with statements of a different category from those with which we began.'[17] The argument has four steps.

(1) 'The first step is to insist that we depend entirely on the premises for our knowledge of the conclusion. Thus it is maintained that we have no access to physical objects otherwise than through the contents of our sense-experiences . . .'

(2) 'The second step in the argument is to show that the relation between premises and conclusion is not deductive. There can be no description of our sense-experiences, however long and detailed, from which it follows that a physical object exists.' Similarly, it can be argued that no statements about theoretical entities are ever deducible from statements about their observable effects, that statements about the thoughts and feelings of other people are never entailed by statements about their overt behaviour, even though such statements describe the only possible evidence, and so on.

(3) But (even if we put aside sceptical doubts about induction itself) there is no acceptable inductive inference to the desired conclusion either. 'Experimental reasoning can carry us forward at a given level; on the basis of certain sense-experiences it allows us to predict the occurrence of other sense-experiences. . . . What it does not permit us is to jump from one level to another; to pass from premises concerning the contents of our sense-

---

[17] Ibid., p. 76

experiences to conclusions about physical objects. . . .'

(4) 'The last step is to argue that since these inferences cannot be justified either deductively or inductively, they cannot be justified at all.'[18]

Arguments which conform to this pattern raise the question of how to justify our inclination to advance beyond our available data in what seems, or is made by the argument to seem, an especially dramatic way. Ayer holds that this problem, or cluster of problems, is what epistemology is all about. 'Concern with the theory of knowledge,' he writes, 'is very much a matter of taking this difficulty seriously'.[19] I think that he is right. Approaching epistemology by way of the sceptical argument allows us to see very clearly what the distinctive features of various epistemological positions are. This constitutes powerful evidence for the view that such theories are best seen as offering different ways of reacting to the threat of radical scepticism.

Ayer sees four main lines of approach to the problem set by the sceptical argument. Naive, or as I shall call it, *direct* realism denies the first step. The direct realist 'will not allow that our knowledge of the various things which the sceptic wishes to put beyond our reach is necessarily indirect'.[20] He holds that physical objects can be directly known.

Classical phenomenalism provides an example of the second approach. This 'reductionist' strategy is to deny the second step. The phenomenalist holds that the gap between data and conclusion which the sceptic makes so much of does not really exist and that the statements about physical objects are analysable into and hence may be entailed by complex statements about sense-experiences. Examples of reductionist theories which apply not globally but to special cases would be logical behaviourism—the theory which

[18] Ibid., pp. 76–78.
[19] Ibid., p. 78.
[20] Ibid., p. 79.

accounts for our knowledge of other minds by claiming that mentalistic discourse is analysable in terms of statements about overt behaviour and dispositions to overt behaviour—and operationalism with respect to the entities postulated by theoretical science.

Thirdly, we have what Ayer calls 'the scientific approach'. This position derives from a denial of the third step of the sceptical argument and claims that, although there is indeed a gap between data and conclusion which needs to be bridged, there is a legitimate form of inductive inference which enables us to bridge it. It is admitted that induction by simple enumeration will not do the job. The basic idea is that, while not directly knowable, physical objects may be known indirectly as the causes of our sensory experience. There are elements of such a view to be found in Hume who thought that the mind postulates 'fictions' to account for the 'constancy and coherence' of sensory experience.[21] Russell, too, once subscribed to a theory of this kind. He held that we infer the existence of physical objects as the simplest explanation of our sensory experience.[22]

It is less easy to see what Ayer's fourth approach amounts to. He calls it 'the method of Descriptive Analysis'. One who adopts this approach will admit that there is a gap between our experiential premises and the claim to knowledge which is our conclusion. He will also admit that this gap cannot be bridged either by induction or deduction. But this does not condemn the inferences we actually make:

> They are what they are, and none the worse for that. Moreover, they can be analysed. We can, for example, show in what conditions we feel confident in attributing certain feelings to others: we can evaluate different types of record: we can distinguish the cases in which our

[21] Hume, *Treatise,* Bk. 1, Pt. IV, Sect. ii. I no longer regard this as a correct account of Hume's argument.

[22] Bertrand Russell, *The Problems of Philosophy* (London: Oxford University Press, 1959), pp. 21-24.

memories or perceptions are taken to be reliable from those in which they are not. In short, we can give an account of the procedures we actually follow. But no justification of those procedures is necessary or possible.[23]

Thus he concludes: 'The sceptic's doubts are insoluble because they are fictitious.'[24]

This is puzzling. Given his previously stated view that concern with the theory of knowledge is very much a matter of taking seriously the problems raised by the radical sceptic, he ought to conclude that the theory of knowledge is just as fictitious as the sceptical problems themselves. Also, the sense in which we are supposed to be unable to evaluate standards of evidence is far from clear.

Ayer is prepared to entertain the view that 'it does not greatly matter whether we regard the need for analysis as superseding the demand for justification, or whether we make the justification consist in the analysis'.[25] The concept of analysis, and the idea that there is a need for analyses to be carried through, are the source of our difficulties. Ayer's claim that 'analysing' consists in describing our actual procedures of justification suggests that to give an analysis would be to make a contribtuion to the sociology or psychology of inquiry; but it is hard to see any epistemological writings, least of all Ayer's own, in this light. And why the *need* for analysis if the problems are fictitious?

Pollock, who follows Ayer closely in this treatment of the problem of perceptual knowledge, uses 'Descriptivism' to refer to the view that statements about how things look constitute logical reasons for judgements about how they really are. Not all logical reasons are deductive reasons.[26]

---

[23] Ayer, op. cit., p. 80.
[24] Ibid., p. 81.
[25] Ibid., p. 83.
[26] John L. Pollock, 'Perceptual Knowledge', *Philosophical Review* (1971), pp. 287-319. For the point in question see pp. 300-302.

The idea here seems to be that it is analytically true—i.e. true in virtue of the meanings of our terms—that certain statements, if justifiably believed, count as good evidence for the truth of certain other kinds of beliefs, even though statements expressing these beliefs cannot be analysed into statements of the evidence-conferring kind. I think that this is what philosophers have in mind when they argue that the connexion between how things look and how they really are, or between behaviour and mental states, is neither straightforwardly deductive nor straightforwardly inductive, but rather criteriological.

This approach to radical scepticism offers the advantages of an appeal to truth in virtue of meaning without the implausibilities of strict reductionism, and I think it is the position to which Ayer himself is led. Thus:

> It is characteristic of what is meant by such a sentence as 'There is a cigarette case on this table' that my having just the experience I am having is evidence for the truth of the statement which it expresses.[27]

In the end, Ayer does not give up on the sceptic's problems. To be sure, he abandons all hope of carrying through any kind of reductive analysis of physical-object statements in terms of statements about sense-experience; but he still answers the sceptic by appealing to evidential connexions which hold in virtue of meaning. Descriptive analysis turns out to be meaning analysis. This position marks a significant retreat from the pessimism about the possibility of epistemology implicit in his initial description of the method.

The value of Ayer's contribution lies in his having exposed the logical structure underlying various 'Cartesian' arguments. Such arguments take the form of raising some bizarre possibility and asking how one could know that it was not actually the case. Thus the question could be raised

[27] Ayer, op. cit., p. 132.

as to how it is possible to know that one is not the victim of some psychological experiment where one is kept alive as a brain in a vat with all one's apparent experience of the physical world artificially induced by direct stimulation. In this example, we are still supposing that something exists that might reasonably be called 'a physical world,' that we have brains, and so on. But perhaps the experiment is being conducted by some totally alien means—by Descartes' evil demon perhaps—and there is no physical world, we don't have brains, or bodies of any kind.

Why should the mere conceivability of such situations, if they are indeed conceivable, make questionable our conviction that we know them not to obtain? If any of them were to obtain, then we should not know much, if anything, that we think we know. But none of them do, so why should our claim to knowledge be impugned?

The point of raising such examples might be to show that, since such possibilities can never be ruled out with absolute conclusiveness, we can never, strictly speaking, know anything about the physical world. For, it might be said, knowing requires being absolutely certain, and we cannot be absolutely certain about our commonsense beliefs if various other bizarre possibilities cannot be conclusively rejected. To take this line would be to argue for one of the weaker forms of scepticism described earlier. Ayer has exposed the structure of Cartesian arguments construed as arguments for radical scepticism. Given that our claims to knowledge of the physical world must find their ultimate justification in a body of epistemologically prior knowledge—generally taken to be whatever knowledge is furnished by immediate experience—the sceptic challenges us to show how this knowledge (supplemented perhaps by knowledge of necessary truth) points towards the beliefs we in fact hold rather than towards alternative hypotheses which seem to be 'empirically equivalent', that is to say, compatible with just the same experiential evidence. Indeed, the sceptic has an argument to show that his challenge cannot be met. But unless the foundational view is assumed, calling attention to Cartesian examples will not generate an argument for radical scepticism. If Moore were allowed just to show us his hands, or Locke allowed to appeal to the science of his day, there would be no problem. Certainly, there would be no call for epistemological theories as we know them.

Ayer's analysis of the sceptical argument allows us to see clearly the distinctive features of various epistemological theories. This is why it is illuminating to see such theories as offering different ways of responding to radical scepticism. But now I wish to enter a caveat. Although there is a lot of merit in Ayer's way of classifying epistemological strategies, it is incomplete as an account of their underlying motivations. He represents different theories as resulting from denying different steps in the sceptical argument, but does not bring out the fact that all the theories share certain crucial assumptions with the argument itself. The last three approaches agree that physical objects are not directly known. The direct realist denies this: he thinks that physical objects can be directly known. But all the approaches agree that *some* things are directly known. Furthermore, they all agree that the question of what can be directly known is, in some sense, a matter of necessity, a matter for philosophical argument rather than empirical inquiry. The common ground between the sceptical argument and all the responses to it is the foundational view of knowledge and justification.

This is an important point. Ayer's way of setting out the problem suggests that his four approaches exhaust the field. But this will be true only if we come up with some good reason for accepting the assumptions common to the four approaches. This is why I say that Ayer's account of different epistemological theories as being different ways of responding to the sceptical argument is incomplete. Because of the framework of shared assumptions, the theories have a certain similarity of structure. We need to know why a theory of this kind has to be correct.

Pollock's account of the task of the epistemologist points towards a similar conclusion. The task of showing how knowledge is possible, given that it is possible, is to proceed by 'giving logical analyses which exhibit a logical connexion between the knowledge claims and the purported grounds of the knowledge claims'.[28] But these 'purported grounds' turn out to be whatever epistemologically prior and, in the end, whatever epistemologically basic knowledge we possess. To sum up, we can say that traditional epistemological theories attempt to show how empirical knowledge may be placed on its proper foundation. Empiricist theories take this foundation to have something to do with sense-perception. It is with theories of this kind that I shall be mainly concerned and that I take, in a broad sense, to be phenomenalistic.

If I am right, the question for us to ask is whether there is any reason to suppose that empirical knowledge needs a foundation. I shall begin, in chapter two, by examining a view closely connected with the foundational picture, to the effect that empirical knowledge results from the interaction of two components: that which is given to sense and the element of construction or interpretation imposed by the mind. Hopefully, an examination of this idea, which lies at the heart of the traditional sense-datum theory, will serve as a useful propaedeutic to the later stages of my argument, for it seems to me that many central themes in phenomenalist thinking are not readily detached from this old-fashioned looking view.

The central concern of chapter three will be to try to see whether there are any compelling reasons for accepting the idea that empirical knowledge rests on a foundation of perceptual knowledge. It has often been thought that unless some knowledge were foundational, nothing else we believe could be justified at all. The basic idea is that not everything

---

[28] Pollock, 'Perceptual Knowledge', p. 287.

we claim to know can be justified by an appeal to further knowledge: there can be no infinite regress of justification. There must, therefore, be some things that we know non-inferentially; there must be epistemologically basic beliefs, beliefs which can be self-justifying, or in some way intrinsically credible, to function as ultimate terminating points for chains of justification. This line of thought I call 'the regress argument'. There are two ways in which it can be taken, although they have not always been carefully distinguished. These are (1) that unless there were basic beliefs, knowledge could not get off the ground—this I call 'the genetic argument'—and (2) that if there were no basic beliefs, one could be 'justified' in believing anything. Empirical knowledge would be, in C. I. Lewis's phrase, 'contentless and arbitrary'. An important claim to consider in this connexion is that to abandon the foundational view of knowledge is to commit oneself to a coherence theory of justification.

We are now in a position to see more clearly why the idea that epistemological theories are best seen as offering different ways of responding to the threat of radical scepticism, where this threat is seen as arising out of the sceptical argument as formulated by Ayer, does not tell the whole story. The threat of scepticism actually arises on two distinct levels. At the first level, it arises to compel the adoption of the foundational view: for the claim that, if there were no epistemologically basic beliefs, knowledge could never get off the ground, or the claim that one would be 'justified' in believing anything at all, threaten us with a scepticism so all-corroding as to truly deserve the epithet 'radical'. This is the level of scepticism with which Chisholm's attempt to uncover the foundations of knowledge through 'Socratic' questioning is concerned. However, having once accepted the idea that there must be a foundation for knowledge, we are faced with the problem of explaining how our chosen foundation could possibly function as such. This is the point at which we seem compelled to choose between the familiar options: direct realism, reductionism (or some other version of the appeal to meaning), and 'the scientific approach'. The task is made pressing by the sceptic's claim that we are doomed to failure. Thus the respite from scepticism afforded by the recognition of epistemologically basic knowledge threatens to be short-lived: for having once accepted the foundational view we become vulnerable to one form or another of the sceptical argument. It seems that in giving knowledge a foundation we also fix its limits, for there is no acceptable inference to carry us beyond the foundation we have set.

One result of all this is that Ayer is quite wrong to claim that the sceptic's problems are fictitious. Once we give in to the idea that empirical knowledge needs to be placed on a foundation, we become vulnerable to sceptical attack. In fact, Ayer's presentation of the sceptical argument does not give an accurate impression of the true strength of the sceptic's assault on the possibility of knowledge. The two major defensive strategies—the appeal to meaning and the scientific approach—are both hopeless. If the burden of the radical sceptic's claim is that any attempt to place empirical knowledge on a foundation is bound to fail, I should say that he is quite right and that this constitutes a powerful reason for thinking that the foundational view must be wrong. Making good this claim will be the topic of chapter four.

In chapter five, I shall complete my argument by asking how there could be such a thing as epistemologically basic knowledge. On the face of it, no belief is self-justifying, or worthy of credence simply in virtue of being held. It is just a fact about human beings that we can make reliable, off-the-cuff reports about some things, though not about others, and it is to such facts that we should look for the justification of claims to 'non-inferential' knowledge. Historically, the idea that there must be some things which are 'directly known' has been closely associated with the idea that some things must be indubitably or incorrigibly known: hence the slogan that if nothing is certain, nothing else is even probable. I shall argue that the popular view tht some beliefs constitute basic knowledge in virtue of being incorrigible rests on a mistake. In my view, this is the rock on which the foundational view of knowledge must eventually founder: that it is quite unintelligible how anything we claim to know could be foundational in the way that the theory requires.

If we can free ourselves from the apparent need to place empirical knowledge on its proper foundation then, clearly, we shall no longer face the philosophical task of choosing and defending one of the traditional theories of how this is to be accomplished. In so far as concern with the theory of knowledge has been a matter of choosing and defending one of these theories, the theory of knowledge will not be something we need concern ourselves with further.

2. The Appeal to the Given

1. INTRODUCTORY REMARKS

Phenomenalism, broadly speaking, is *the* empiricist theory of perceptual knowledge. Classical phenomenalism is the theory that physical objects are logical constructions out of sense-data. In a more explicitly linguistic guise, it is the theory that the content of any statement about physical objects can be expressed by some complex statement about sense-data. The classical theory has few adherents, if any, these days.[1] Reference to sense-data has been replaced by talk about how one is appeared to, and the idea that sufficiently complex statements about perceptual experience might *entail* statements about how things are in the physical world has given way to the idea that the connexion is *criteriological.* But these modifications do not touch the basic idea behind phenomenalism which is that there are epistemologically basic beliefs which are in some way perceptual beliefs and which serve as a foundation—or at least as a partial foundation—for our beliefs about the physical world.

The foundational role of perceptual beliefs was something we found to be presupposed by Ayer's formulation of the sceptical argument and by the various responses to it. Even Ayer's version of direct realism accepts the idea of there being a foundation for knowledge, though the foundations

[1] A possible exception is Jonathan Bennett. See his *Locke, Berkeley, Hume.*

stand at a higher level than they do for, say, the sense-datum theory.

According to the usage I am proposing, any theory which assigns a foundational role to perceptual beliefs of one kind or another deserves to be called 'phenomenalistic'. By this standard, even some forms of direct realism could be taken to be phenomenalist in spirit. I am aware that this marks a departure from normal usage. I adopt it because I want to emphasize the important continuities of thought which exist between various theories often taken to be implacable opponents.

For the time being, I shall leave the notion of a foundational role in relative obscurity. I do this because I think that it can best be understood by following through the arguments for the existence of foundations rather than through an attempt to present an encapsulating definition. But before turning to this task, I want to investigate some of the complexities to be found in the traditional sense-datum theory, and this will involve coming to grips with the idea that there is a given element in experience. An examination of some of these older ideas should stand us in good stead for the more general discussion of phenomenalism to come later since, as I shall argue, modern expressions of phenomenalist thought often turn out to be not-so-new variations on the old themes.

2. THE TWO COMPONENTS IN KNOWLEDGE

The expression 'the given' owes much of its philosophical currency to C. I. Lewis's influential book *Mind and the World Order*,[2] and to H. H. Price's *Perception*.[3] The idea that there is a given element in experience reflects one side of

[2] C. I. Lewis, *Mind and the World Order* (New York: Dover, 1956; originally published by Scribners, New York, 1929).

[3] H. H. Price, *Perception* (London: Methuen, reprinted 1964).

a distinction which Lewis regarded as 'one of the oldest and most universal of philosophical insights'. He put the point like this:

> There are in our cognitive experience, two elements, the immediate data such as those of sense, which are presented or given to the mind, and a form, construction, or interpretation, which represents the activity of thought.[4]

I shall call the view that Lewis is alluding to 'the two components view'. He is surely right that epistemological theories embodying a distinction along the above lines have had a long run of philosophical popularity. The two components of knowledge are the sensuously given and the pure concept. The distinction drawn by Lewis is clearly related to the distinction between analytic truths —propositions which are true in virtue of meaning and hence a priori—and synthetic truths, which are dependent on matters of fact. As Lewis puts it, '. . . the concept gives rise to the a priori; all a priori truth is definitive, or explicative of concepts.'[5]

What are the philosophical reasons for continuing to recognize a distinction like this? Lewis thought that there was no question that such a distinction had to be recognized. To deny that there was a distinction between the given and its interpretation would be to turn one's back on obvious and fundamental characteristics of experience. Thus he argued:

> If there be no datum given to the mind, then knowledge must be altogether contentless and arbitrary; there would be nothing which it must be true to. And if there be no interpretation which the mind imposes, then thought is rendered superfluous, the possibility of error becomes

[4] Lewis, op. cit., p. 38.
[5] Ibid., p. 37.

inexplicable, and the distinction of true and false is in danger of becoming meaningless.[6]

It is not difficult to see what Lewis is getting at. Our knowledge of the physical world must have a foundation in perception or observation. It cannot all be a matter of theorizing or of inference: there must be some data on the basis of which to theorize or make inferences, if the result of such activity is not to be 'contentless and arbitrary'. This basic knowledge is certain because absolutely non-inferential: thus we have a permanent data-base of observational knowledge against which less guarded claims can be evaluated. That empirical knowledge as we understand it goes beyond what is given, and hence involves thought or inference, is shown by the fact that we allow for the possibility of error. If thought never ventured beyond what is given, error would never arise. And we find a similar view in Price's book. If we are to have inferential knowledge, he argues, we must ultimately be able to appeal to some data which are 'data simpliciter', otherwise there would be a vicious regress.[7]

What we have here are not 'obvious characteristics' of experience, but rather a highly compressed philosophical argument, one which I shall discuss in some detail in chapter three. For the time being, I wish to concentrate more on the question of what the distinction between the sensuously given and its interpretation is supposed to be.

Since the apprehension of the given element is supposed to provide the ultimate check upon empirical knowledge, it must itself be some form of primitive knowledge or awareness. But when we recall the sharp distinction drawn between the pure concept and the sensuously given, a problem arises. The pure concept and the sensuously given

[6] Ibid., p. 39.
[7] Price, op. cit., p. 4. But see the whole of chapter 1.

are thought by Lewis to be mutually independent—'neither limits the other'—but this makes it look as if the mind has to be able to grasp the given without conceptual mediation. In other words, the knowledge which is involved in the grasping of the sensuously given, since it is independent of conceptual interpretation by the mind, must be non-propositional or, to put the point more pejoratively, ineffable. But if it is ineffable, it cannot provide us with a check upon anything, let alone the entire edifice of empirical knowledge.

To illustrate the problem, we may consider for a moment the idealist attack on the notion of givenness. The doctrine of the given has acquired an association with empiricism. This is reflected by the fact that attacks on the notion of givenness have tended to concentrate, as I shall do, on empiricist versions of the theory. It is not uncommon to find the positions taken by those who would call in question the two components view described as idealist positions. I think that this is a mistake. Furthermore, it can be an important mistake in that it can lead one to think that one is rejecting the whole idea of givenness when one is only rejecting a particular empiricist version.

Lewis clearly believed that any adequate epistemological theory must start from the distinction between the given and its interpretation. Thus, although idealists have often seemed to be attacking givenness at large, Lewis argued, correctly in my judgment, that they never really meant to say that *nothing* is given. What they were opposed to were certain ways of characterizing the given element in experience.

The seeming hostility shown by idealists towards talk of givenness springs from their taking the distinction between the active and passive faculties of the mind even more seriously than many of their philosophical opponents. If thought is equated with activity and the apprehension of the sensuously given with passive receptivity, we cannot consistently treat the kind of awareness involved in apprehending the contents of the given as being nevertheless a kind of thinking—i.e. a form of propositional knowledge. This is the point underlying Bradley's insistence that all cognition is judgment and that what many philosophers have taken to be data could not really be data because awareness of them already involves conceptualization. It is a point which idealists have been fond of using against empiricists and is, for example, brought up again and again by Green in his polemic against Locke and Hume.[8] But although Bradley insists, in the interests of consistency, that whatever is given can be nothing *for the intellect,* he does not dismiss the notion of givenness altogether. Rather, he is led to characterize the given as a kind of undifferentiated immediate experience in which the distinction between subject and object has not yet emerged. According to Bradley, the given is 'experienced altogether as a coexisting mass, not perceived as parted and joined even by relations of coexistence'.[9] However, in spite of the ineffable character of immediate experience, the content of which we know only as 'this', he holds that 'all our knowledge, in the first place, arises from the "this". It is the one source of our experience, and every element of the world must submit to pass through it.'[10]

Bradley's position is apt to strike one as merely ridiculous. But it is ridiculous just because his conception of immediate experience respects rigidly the distinction between the sensuously given and the element of thought or interpretation which he sees must be involved in anything that could be called cognition. Bradley's position must be taken as a reductio ad absurdum of the concept of givenness precisely because it throws into sharp relief a dilemma which

[8] T. H. Green, the introduction to his edition of Hume's works. Reprinted as *Thomas Hill Green's Hume and Locke* (New York: Apollo, 1968).
[9] F. H. Bradley, *Appearance and Reality* (Oxford: Clarendon Press, paperback edition 1969), p. 198.
[10] Ibid., p. 198.

ultimately confronts any consistent 'two elements in knowledge' view. The dilemma is this: that in so far as the content of immediate experience can be expressed, the sort of awareness we have in our apprehension of the given is just another type of perceptual judgment and hence no longer contact with anything which is *merely given*. But if the content of immediate experience turns out to be ineffable or non-propositional, then the appeal to the given loses any appearance of fulfilling an explanatory role in the theory of knowledge: specifically, it cannot explicate the idea that knowledge rests on a perceptual foundation. This, it seems to me, is why, after we have learned that we are aware in immediate experience only of 'a coexisting mass', the insistence that this kind of awareness is the source of all our experience and that 'every element of the world must submit to pass through it' strikes us as extraordinarily futile.

3. NON-PROPOSITIONAL KNOWLEDGE

If the given is seen as that which is received passively and independently of the constructive activity of thought, it is difficult to resist the conclusion that the content of the given is fundamentally ineffable. It is difficult to avoid letting the given element in experience dwindle away to something along the lines of Bradley's immediate experience. Thus Lewis comes surprisingly close to Bradley on this point:

> . . . we cannot describe any particular given as such, because in describing it, in whatever fashion, we qualify it by bringing it under some category or other, select from it, emphasise aspects of it, and relate it in particular and avoidable ways.[11]

Empiricists have a particular stake in taking the kind of

[11] Lewis, op. cit., p. 52.

knowledge or awareness which is involved in our encounter with the sensuously given to be ineffable or, which comes to the same thing, non-propositional. It comes from their characteristic insistence that conceptual abilities, especially those which come with the learning of a language, need to be acquired.[12] Since experience of the sensuously given is something we have simply in virtue of being conscious, such experience must be independent of any particular conceptual abilities and cannot be taken to presuppose the possession of any such abilities. Indeed, confrontation with the given is often taken to be part of the explanation of how certain primitive linguistic abilities are acquired: this is the theory that certain 'basic' predicates are learned 'ostensively'.

Further pressure to make the content of awareness of the given non-propositional comes from the requirement that the given provide a rock-bottom level of certainty to which to anchor empirical knowledge. If awareness of the sensuously given turned out to be one more variety of perceptual judgment, the certainty of the given would seem to be threatened. For describing is not an activity which brings with it a logical guarantee of success. However, to yield to this pressure results in a pyrrhic victory. The certainty of the given is saved only at the cost of making it unintelligible how awareness of the given could serve as a check on anything, how such knowledge could ever count in favour of one hypothesis rather than another. The appeal to the given is not going to save knowledge from being 'contentless and arbitrary'.

Price considers an objection to the notion of givenness which he calls 'the a priori thesis'.[13] The objection is that

[12] The process of acquisition must, of course, be seen as one of conscious learning rather than one of training. The alternative to this kind of empiricism is not a doctrine of innate ideas, though it might be a doctrine of innate predispositions to respond more readily to some stimuli than to others. My views on these matters are much influenced by Wittgenstein.

[13] Price, op. cit., p. 6.

nothing can ever be given since it is impossible to apprehend something without apprehending some of its qualities and relations. Price's reply is that this is very likely true, but irrelevant. At most, the argument proves that nothing stands merely in the relation of givenness to the mind, but it does not show that nothing is given. Lewis, too, is prepared to admit that the given is 'an abstraction'. However, this does not meet the objection we are developing which is that, once the concept of the given is emasculated in the way that these various difficulties require, it no longer holds out the promise of fulfilling an explanatory role in the theory of knowledge. Price has some reasons of his own for not anticipating this reply. We shall come to these shortly.

In fact, the doctrine of the ineffability of the given is impossible to maintain. Necessarily, it breaks down when one attempts to give some characterization of the given whereby it is to be distinguished from other elements in experience. Building on the idea that the given is the element in experience shared by all conscious beings, no matter what their peculiar conceptual accomplishments, Lewis offers 'unalterability' as the criterion for givenness:

> My designation of this thing as 'pen' reflects my purpose to write; as 'cylinder' my desire to explain a problem in geometry or mechanics; as 'a poor buy' my resolution to be more careful hereafter in my expenditures. . . . The distinction between this element of interpretation and the given is emphasised by the fact that the latter is what remains unaltered, no matter what our interests, no matter how we think or conceive. I can apprehend this thing as pen or rubber or cylinder, but I cannot, by taking thought, discover it as paper or soft or cubical.[14]

Lewis here implies that the pen is given as non-soft, non-cubical, non-paper and thereby offers at least three

14 Lewis, op. cit., p. 52.

descriptions of the content of the given. To illustrate the notion of the given by contrasting different descriptions is to contradict the idea that the content of the given is ineffable.

The doctrine of non-propositional knowledge associated with the two components view has its roots in an attempt to hold simultaneously to two conceptions of the given. The idea that the given constitutes the sensuous element in experience strongly suggests that particular things are given, such things as colour patches, Lewis's qualia and so on. But the theoretical role which the concept of givenness is called upon to play requires that taking the given amount to acquiring non-inferential knowledge. That these two views must prove difficult to combine should be apparent. Surely, whatever can be known must be the sort of thing which can be true or false, a condition not met by the data of sense conceived as phenomenal objects.

Russell's discussion of sense-data in *The Problems of Philosophy* illustrates nicely how easy it is to confuse these two conceptions of the given. He is commendably aware that sense-data, if regarded as coloured patches in the visual field, cannot be bearers of truth-values. Thus:

> . . . The actual sense-data are neither true nor false. A particular patch of colour, which I see, for example, simply exists: it is not the sort of thing which is true or false. It is true that there is such a patch, true that it has a certain shape and a certain degree of brightness, true that it is surrounded by certain other colours. But the patch itself is of a radically different kind from the things that are true or false, and therefore cannot properly be said to be *true*.[15]

This   means   that   our   'knowledge'   of   sense-data—

---

[15] Bertrand Russell, *The Problems of Philosophy* (New York: Galaxy edition, O.U.P., 1969), p. 113.

acquaintance—must be sharply distinguished from factual knowledge:

> . . . We shall say that we have *acquaintance* with anything of which we are directly aware without the intermediary of any process of inference or any knowledge of truths. Thus in the presence of my table I am acquainted with the sense-data that make up the appearance of the table—its colour, shape, hardness, smoothness, etc.; all these are things of which I am immediately conscious when I am seeing and touching my table. The particular shade of colour that I am seeing may have many things said about it—I may say that it is brown, that it is rather dark, and so on. But such statements, though they may make known truths *about* the colour, do not make me know the colour itself any better than I did before: so far as concerns knowledge of the colour itself, as opposed to knowledge of truths about it, I know the colour perfectly and completely when I see it and no further knowledge of it itself is even theoretically possible.[16]

So far, so good, though even here, I would argue, the looseness of Russell's language betrays uncertainty as to whether acquaintance presents us with a particular shade of colour, in the sense of a determinate shade of colour, or with a particular which is thus coloured. The latter is what he ought to mean, in which case his inability to acquire further knowledge of the sense-datum is on a par with Alice's inability to accept more tea from the March Hare. But more revealing still is the conclusion he draws from his characterization of acquaintance, a conclusion which encapsulates his account of how acquaintance, a relation between a subject and a particular phenomenal object, can nevertheless yield knowledge:

[16] Ibid., pp. 46-47.

... Thus the sense-data which make up the appearance of my table are things with which I have acquaintance, things immediately known to me just as they are.[17]

So when I am acquainted with sense-data they are known to me *just as they are*—that is, presumably, as brown, square or whatever. But how is this having knowledge of the datum as brown and square to be distinguished from knowing *that it is brown and square?* The difference is entirely verbal: the uncertainty has been resolved and acquaintance with objects quietly transformed into factual 'knowing that'.

We find similar confusion in Price's discussion of sense-data, though his argument moves in the opposite direction. His initial attempt to determine what is given leads him to an allegedly indubitable perceptual judgment—that he is presented with something red and bulgy. But from there on it is taken as established that 'sense-data' are given and that the givenness of these peculiar objects is somehow prior to any factual knowledge.

Now because the givenness of sense-data, on one of its faces, is the givenness of things not of facts, we can see why the content of the given tends towards the ineffable. The ineffability of the given springs from the fact that, in one sense, the taking of the given involves no judgment, no commitment to any factual claim whatsoever. But by the same token the sense in which the given is immune from error is without epistemological significance. There is nothing to be wrong about, but nothing to be right about either.

Russell's phrase 'knowledge by acquaintance' suggests that the idea of non-propositional knowledge might take comfort from our colloquial talk of knowing people and places and not just facts. This is a mistake. Our acquaintance

---

[17] Ibid., p. 47.

with people and places, unlike our alleged acquaintance with sense-data, is not independent of and logically prior to any factual knowledge about them. Indeed, a moment's consideration will show that the analogy between our 'acquaintance' with (= sensing of) sense-data and our acquaintance with people and places is not at all close. The sensing of sense-data is a mental act, whereas knowing Paris is a dispositional state. I can know Paris without being confronted with the place, whereas it is agreed on all hands that acquaintance with a sense-datum requires the presence of the datum before the mind. Neither does my knowing Paris imply that I know it well. However, although these matters are not entirely uncontroversial, the consensus view has been that acquaintance with sense-data is not something that can go badly. Ayer thought that it did not make sense to suppose that sense-data could appear to be other than as they are, and Russell thought that when I am acquainted with a red sense-datum, my knowledge of the colour itself could not be improved upon, even in principle. By contrast, talk of 'knowledge of Paris itself' (as opposed to knowledge of any facts about the place) which could not be improved upon, even in principle, would not even make sense. Our every-day use of 'acquaintance' does not help generate any understanding whatsoever of the use of that term to designate a kind of non-propositional knowledge which underpins all factual knowledge.

The notion of non-propositional knowledge by ac-quaintance is, then, a technical notion and a confused one at that. The idea that particulars are given leads to the conclusion that being acquainted with a sense-datum is not an epistemic fact at all. That is to say, acquaintance with a sense-datum does not imply the acquisition of non-inferential knowledge. But acquaintance with the given element in experience has to be shown to constitute or at least imply the acquisition of such knowledge or the appeal to the given loses its point. The concept of non-propositional knowledge can be seen as the product of these conflicting tendencies in the sense-datum theory.

Is there any way for a sense-datum theorist to combine the ideas that phenomenal particulars are given and that nevertheless our sensing of them constitutes a kind of knowledge? Sellars has suggested that he must say something like the following:

> The non-inferential knowing on which our world-picture rests is the knowing that certain items, e.g. red sense-contents, are of a certain character, e.g. red. When such a fact is non-inferentially known about a sense-content, I will say that it is sensed as being e.g. red. I will then say that a sense-content is sensed (full stop) if it is sensed *as being* of a certain character, e.g. red. Finally, I will say of a sense-content that it is known if it is sensed (full stop), to emphasise the fact that sensing is a cognitive or epistemic fact.[18]

As Sellars points out, these stipulations make it logically necessary that 'if a sense-content be *sensed,* it be sensed *as being* of a certain character and that if it be *sensed as being* of a certain character, the *fact that it is* of that character be non-inferentially known'.[19]

Although this seems at first sight to be what we wanted, it should be clear that the stipulative introduction of new senses for 'know' and other epistemic terms is really a

[18] Wilfrid Sellars, 'Empiricism and the Philosophy of Mind', in Feigl and Scrivens (eds.), *Minnesota Studies in the Philosophy of Science*, Vol. 1. Reprinted as ch. 5 of Sellars' *Science, Perception and Reality* (London: Routledge, Kegan Paul, 1963). All references to this edition. In my judgment, Sellars' article is one of the most important philosophical pieces published on this subject and I have been strongly influenced by his critique of empiricism. Unfortunately, like so many things by Sellars, it is often difficult to follow. I think that this is why his work frequently fails to get the recognition it deserves. Quotation, p. 129.

[19] Ibid., pp. 129–30.

pointless manoeuvre. Sellars writes as if maintaining the logical connection between sensing sense-data and non-inferentially knowing some fact to be the case were all that mattered to the sense-datum theorist. This is not so: the sensing of or acquaintance with sense-data is supposed to explain or otherwise underpin the non-inferential knowledge on which all further knowledge is supposed to rest. However, the stipulated 'senses' of 'know' and 'sense' offer nothing more than bits of shorthand, abbreviations for the more conventional locutions of which they are the stipulated equivalents. Thus from the fact that someone stipulates that he will *say* that a sense-content is sensed whenever some fact about it is non-inferentially known, we cannot conclude that he is committed to there being, say, an act of sensing whose unvarying excellence, immediacy and so forth explains how this kind of knowledge is possible or which guarantees its privileged epistemic status. For to say that such a content is sensed is simply to say in abbreviated form that some such fact is known. To put the point in a slightly different way, there can be no warrant for giving a referential interpretation to a term like 'sensing' in such locutions as 'I am now sensing a red sense-content' since the predicate 'x senses a red sense-content' is introduced whole as the stipulated equivalent of 'x non-inferentially knows that a given sense-content is red'. We cannot, therefore, see the stipulatively introduced predicate as having any semantically significant internal structure. No new mental act has been either postulated or discovered.

Of course, Sellars himself is no friend of the sense-datum theory. However, the chief pitfall he sees for a sense-datum theorist who adopts the strategy under consideration lies in the possibility of failing to realize clearly that the fact that a sense-content is given (if there are such facts) will logically imply that someone has non-inferential knowledge only if 'to say that a sense-content is given is contextually defined in terms of non-inferential knowledge of a fact about this sense-content'.[20] Such a failure might induce a tendency 'to think of the givenness of sense-data as the basic or primitive concept of the sense-datum framework and thus sever the logical connection between sense-data and non-inferential knowledge to which the classical form of the theory is committed.'[21] True enough, but if a sense-datum theorist cannot take the givenness of sense-data to be the basic concept of his theoretical framework then he has no theoretical framework to speak of. It is odd that Sellars should consider the conventionalist strategy he discusses to be a device by means of which a sense-datum theorist might try to save his position from incoherence since, as we shall see, the objection I have been developing is very similar to one advanced by Sellars himself against the 'alternative language' account of the sense-datum theory.

In view of all this, perhaps it would be better for a sense-datum theorist to claim that talk about acquaintance with sense-data is introduced not by mere verbal stipulation but rather *theoretically* to explain our possession of a specially privileged kind of knowledge. The introduction of sense-data is thus effected by what is sometimes called an inference to the best explanation: they are theoretical entities postulated for explanatory purposes in epistemology. This seems the most promising line for the sense-datum theorist to take. As many writers have pointed out, all the standard arguments in favour of sense-data fail if intended to be deductively valid; and it is faithful to the idea that the sensibly given constitutes one of the fundamental categories of the theory of knowledge.

There are a number of things to be said about this suggestion. Perhaps the most obvious is that, far from being the best explanation for the fact that the judgment that there looks to me to be something red in front of me now appears much more 'certain' than the judgment that there is a red

[20] Ibid., p. 130.
[21] Ibid., p. 130.

tomato in front of me now, the sense-datum theory is quite unnecessarily complex. The greater 'certainty' of the one judgment is adequately accounted for by the fact that it makes a much weaker claim than the other. However, a more fundamental objection can be raised, and this is to question whether the sense-datum theory has any explanatory force at all. Basic perceptual knowledge is thought to be certain and non-inferential because it arises out of our sensing of or acquaintance with sense-data; and sensing is generally thought to be 'unvaryingly excellent', its objects 'cannot appear to be other than as they are'. But as soon as we look a little more closely at this explanation, our old problem re-emerges. If acquaintance or sensing is a relation between a subject and a particular object which involves no 'abstraction' or description, as Lewis and Price insist, and hence, as Russell points out, no knowledge of truths, how does our acquaintance with the sensibly given explain our possessing non-inferential knowledge? Russell, for example, tells us that if someone is acquainted with a thing which exists, his acquaintance gives him knowledge that it exists, but he does not tell us how, only that this state which involves no knowledge of truths 'gives' us knowledge of a truth. The connection between the given element in experience and empirical knowledge remains obscure. Of course, there remains the possibility already noted of making the connection simply by transforming our acquaintance with sense-data into the right kind of knowledge of truths, but this leaves us with the merest pretence of an explanatory theory.

To sum up, the concept of non-propositional knowledge represents a confused attempt to combine the idea that phenomenal particulars are given with the conflicting idea that our relation to these particulars must amount to a kind of non-inferential knowledge. But although in this section we have been concerned with older expositions of the sense-datum theory, the problems we have encountered lie at the heart of phenomenalist theories, even in my broad sense, and we shall meet them again. In fact, the errors into which sense-datum theorists have commonly fallen can tempt a philosopher with no wish to defend any version of phenomenalism. For example, a recent writer has argued that the existence of 'Gettier examples' in perception shows that even direct perceptual knowledge must be based on inference.[22] Having rejected the idea that there is a sensory given to function as a basis for this inference on the grounds that the way things appear to us is to a considerable extent affected by further beliefs and expectations, he is led to identify the basic data with sensory stimulations: not with beliefs about such stimulations since, obviously, we rarely entertain such beliefs, but, in the case of visual perception, with the physical patterns of stimulation on the retina which function as non-linguistic representations. As premises for an inference, these neurophysiological events are just as inappropriate as Russell's sense-data or Bradley's immediate experience knowable only as 'this', and for the same reason: that is, they are not the kind of things which could be true or false. For all its up-to-date appearance, this recent view is no improvement on the sense-datum theory.[23]

[22] Gilbert Harman, *Thought* (Princeton, 1973), ch. 11.

A Gettier example is a situation in which we have justified true belief but not 'knowledge': e.g. at four o'clock I look at the clock on the wall and see that it points to four o'clock. The clock keeps good time, I have no reason to suspect that there is anything wrong with it, and so my belief that it is four o'clock is both justified and true. But unknown to me, the clock has stopped: it is pure luck that I happen to glance at the clock just when its hands are pointing to the right time. In this case, some would argue, I could not be said to *know* that it is four o'clock.

[23] Harman would reply that these sensory stimulations count as non-linguistic representations in virtue of their function in guiding action and leading to belief. I rather doubt whether this really justifies calling retinal stimulations 'representations' but, even if it did, the problem would not be solved since these stimulations, now elevated to the status of representations, would still not be appropriate as premises for an inference.

4. FINDING THE GIVEN

The lesson to be learned from Bradley seemed to be that if you try to take the two components view seriously, you end up casting doubt on the validity and theoretical utility of the distinctions on which the view depends. But some philosophers would hold that to deny the existence of the given on the grounds that the appeal to the given is of doubtful theoretical utility would be to take an incorrect view of what is at issue.[24] Price, for example, thought that since sense-data were given, it was hard to see how anyone could doubt their existence. All that the philosopher could do when faced with an unbeliever would be to remove any mistaken objections which might stand in the way of that person's taking an unbiased look at the contents of perceptual consciousness. This suggests that the dispute between the various advocates of givenness about what was actually given was a matter for introspective psychology to clear up.[25] The relevance of epistemological considerations seems obscure.

Moore, too, offered directions for 'pointing out' sense-data. The idea was that one should take a look at one's hand and pick out something that one would naturally take to be identical with the surface of one's hand but which might turn out not to be.[26]

In fact, Price's practice belied his theory. For he did not discover sense-data simply by taking an unbiased introspective look at the contents of his perceptual consciousness. Rather he adopted the sophisticated device of placing himself in a perceptual situation—that of looking at

[24] For example, Benson Mates has tried to show that sense-data exist without getting embroiled in epistemological issues. See his article, 'Sense-Data', *Inquiry*, 10 (1967), pp. 225-244.

[25] Price, op. cit., p. 5.

[26] G. E. Moore, 'The Defence of Common Sense', *Contemporary British Philosophy*, Second Series (London: Allen and Unwin, 1925).

a tomato under normal conditions of illumination, etc.—and then trying to discover which of the beliefs he was inclined to form in that situation could possibly be doubted. He was not interested in mere subjective feelings of conviction: he asked, in effect, what could theoretically be doubted. This procedure is epistemological through and through and takes him close to Moore whose method for picking out sense-data was less naive than one might at first suppose. As Moore later admitted,[27] his procedure was founded on the assumption that, whether there is any physical object there or not when I attempt to look at my hand, there is nevertheless *something* which is seen in that special sense of 'see' which Moore called 'direct apprehension'.

Here are the results of Price's thought-experiment:

> One thing however I cannot doubt: that there exists a red patch of a round and somewhat bulgy shape, standing out from a background of other colour-patches, and having a certain visual depth, and that this whole field of colour is directly present to my consciousness. . . . This peculiar manner of being present to consciousness is called *being given* and that which is thus present is called a *datum.* The corresponding mental attitude is called *acquaintance, intuitive apprehension,* or sometimes *having.*[28]

It is often said that Price is here advancing an argument for the claim that we have direct knowledge only of sense-data. The argument, sometimes called the Argument from Differential Certainty, is to the effect that since I cannot doubt that I am presented with a red patch but can doubt that I am presented with a tomato, it must be the red patch, now to be called a sense-datum, and not the tomato, that is

---

[27] G. E. Moore, 'Reply to my Critics', in P. Schilpp (ed.), *The Philosophy of G. E. Moore,* Library of Living Philosophers (New York: Tudor, second edition, 1952), p. 632.

[28] Price, op. cit., p. 3.

'directly present to consciousness'. Of course, the argument is invalid and would not be greatly improved even if buttressed by the implausible Platonic principle that judgments possessing radically different degrees of certainty must be about radically different kinds of things. And, indeed, bad as it is, some such argument may be required if Price is to make the move from an indubitable perceptual judgment to a special kind of thing which is the object of that judgment. But an interesting feature of Price's experiment is that he hardly presents it as an *argument* at all. Rather, he begins by presenting what looks like an argument but ends up writing as if what he has really done is describe a procedure for getting ourselves in the right frame of mind to identify introspectively the mental attitude of acquaintance and the data which are its objects.

Now, as I have already suggested, I do not think that we can take this seriously. Price does not really *discover* the mental attitude of acquaintance; he knows in advance that it must exist. For, he says,

> . . . there must be some sort or sorts of presence to consciousness which can be called 'direct' . . . else we should have an infinite regress.[29]

His deep, and unexamined, reasons for accepting the concept of the given element in experience are very close to Lewis's. The given element is not just found: philosophers are led to it by methods which reflect sophisticated epistemological presuppositions.

To add to this, there may be an even shorter way of showing that the given could not be identified introspectively. Evidence from the psychology of perception all points to there being no such thing as a state of sensuous apprehension utterly unaffected by beliefs, desires and

[29] Ibid., p. 3.

expectations and consequently no experience of the given as such. Lewis clearly admits as much when he says that 'any Kantian manifold as a psychic datum or moment of experience is probably a fiction'.[30] And, as we saw earlier, even Price seems to take this line in his response to the a priori thesis.

Even so, the idea that the given element in experience should be identifiable introspectively is not silly. On the contrary, it is strongly suggested by the fact that this element has to be *given*. It is not surprising that Price should find the denial that there are sense-*data* so perplexing. And, looked at in this light, the idea considered in the preceding section that sense-data might be introduced theoretically can seem equally odd: how could theoretical entities be *given*?

There is another way in which the idea that the given is simply discovered by internal inspection is important. Sellars suggests that a sense-datum theorist who stipulatively introduces new senses for 'know' or 'sense' through contextual definitions couched in terms of non-inferential knowledge—and we saw that the sense-datum theory does not amount to much more than this even if we attempt to construe it another way—might still be tempted to take the sensing of sense-data to be the primitive concept of his theoretical framework. The tendency to think that sensing must be an introspectible act and sense-data its intro-spectively identifiable objects is the most potent source of such temptation and lends the concepts of 'sensing' and 'sense-data' an air of independent life which otherwise they simply would not have.

5. The Alternative Language Thesis

There is a view of the appeal to the given and of the sense-

---

[30] Lewis, op. cit., p. 55.

datum theory, associated primarily with A. J. Ayer and G. A. Paul, to the effect that questions and problems arising out of disputes about what is given are not substantive factual questions but rather verbal questions to be settled by fixing the use of expressions in the sense-datum language. Thus:

> The philosopher who says that he is seeing a sense-datum in a case where most people would say that they were perceiving a material object is not contradicting the received opinion on any question of fact. He is not putting forward a new hypothesis which could be empirically verified or confuted. What he is doing is simply recommending a new verbal usage.[31]

Paul does not deal with the question of why anyone should want to introduce the terminology of sense-data in the first place; but Ayer claims to have good philosophical reasons for talking about sense-data, which are essentially that the terminology of sense-data enables us to discuss the facts about sense-perception which are of interest to the philosopher in a clear and illuminating way.

In a vague sort of way, it is not hard to see why this view of philosophical theories of perception has a certain appeal. Ayer calls attention to the fact that philosophical disputes about perception are not readily resolved on empirical grounds and do not seem to make predictions about the future course of experience in the way that scientific theories do. Given a pragmatic view of scientific theories, it is tempting to say that, since the various philosophical theories of perception do not give rise to different empirically testable predictions about the future course of experience, then we are not presented with different *theories* at all. I think that

[31] A. J. Ayer, *The Foundations of Empirical Knowledge* (London: Macmillan, 1940; references to St. Martin's Library Edition, New York, 1964), p. 25.

intuitions like this account for the prima-facie appeal of Ayer's thesis.

But there is another source of its appeal—one which bears directly on our recent discussion. That is, Ayer's thesis offers a comfortable halfway house between the position that sense-data are simply discovered by introspection and the position which takes them to be theoretical entities postulated for explanatory purposes in psychology or the theory of knowledge. As we have seen, it is very difficult to take seriously the idea that sense-data can just be found by introspection. On the other hand, that they should be discoverable in this straightforward way is, as Price saw, strongly suggested by the fact that sense-data, whatever they are, are supposed to be given or directly apprehended. This requirement seems clearly to imply that talk about sense-data belongs to a level of discourse about as untheoretical as you can get.

The upshot of this is that the sense-datum theorist is caught in a dilemma. The view that sense-data are simply discovered by introspecting one's perceptual consciousness is highly implausible. But the alternative view—that they are postulated theoretical entities—seems to conflict with the requirement that they be *given*. Ayer's idea that sense-datum theorists are advocating a new and philosophically useful terminology—in which technical terms like 'direct awareness' or 'sense-datum' are given a stipulated meaning—but are not postulating a new class of entities appears to offer a way between the horns.

Unfortunately, the alternative language thesis looks less appealing when we try to make clear what it really amounts to. How can we make sense of the idea that there is no factual matter at issue between the advocates of sense-data and philosophers who are quite happy with our everyday 'physical object' language? According to Paul:

We so use language that whenever it is true that I am

seeing the round top surface of a penny, and know that it is round, it is true to say that this penny *looks* (e.g.) elliptical to me, in a sense in which this does not entail that I am in any way deceived about the real shape of the penny. (I shall indicate this sense by means of a suffix: 'looks*'.) The rule which has generally been adopted is that the sense-datum is correctly said to have whatever shape and colour-property the corresponding surface of the physical object looks* to me to have.[32]

The idea seems to be that sentences of the form of

(A)   S senses a Ø sense-datum

are stipulated to have the same meaning as sentences of the form of

(B)   It looks to S as though there were a Ø object before him.

Or something like that. The upshot of this seems to be that the terminology of sense-data offers nothing more than notational variants of sentences we would normally construct with the terminology of physical objects looking to observers to be some way or other. This is Sellars' interpretation of the alternative language thesis. The advantage of this interpretation is that it gives a clear sense to the claim that advocating the introduction of the sense-datum terminology does not imply any disagreement about the facts of perception, or that there are any such facts which cannot be captured by our usual way of speaking. The disadvantage of this interpretation is that it makes the thesis quite uninteresting and leaves very unclear why anyone should ever have taken it seriously.

[32] G. A. Paul, 'Is There a Problem about Sense-Data?' *Proceedings of the Aristotelian Society,* Supplementary Volume XV (1936). Reprinted in R. J. Swartz (ed.), *Perceiving, Sensing and Knowing* (New York: Anchor Books, 1965), p. 277.

Some notational devices are very illuminating. It is often much easier to grasp the logical interrelations between complex sentences if they are put into the notation of standard quantificational logic, for example. But it is clear that no such advantages can be expected from the adoption of the sense-datum terminology. In the case of quantificational logic, we have a complete syntax with rules for constructing sentences of any degree of complexity out of elements taken from a fixed number of primitive grammatical categories. Thus it makes sense to talk of translating sentences of English into logical notation. The sense-datum terminology, on the other hand, is introduced by stipulation on a sentence by sentence basis, and this means that the apparent logical structure of sentences of the form of (A) will be merely apparent. From (A), it is not even legitimate to infer

(C)   There are ∅ sense-data

without some further stipulation to fix the meaning of sentences of that form. This is because sentences of the form of (A) are simply stipulated equivalents of sentences of the form of (B). Not merely do no sentences of the form of (C) obviously follow from any sentences of the form of (B); the former have not even been assigned any meaning. But because sense-datum 'sentences' draw on words which are homonyms of words in everyday use, the sense-datum terminology carries with it the constant danger of leading us into false inferences by suggesting logical structure where there is really none to be found, and by obscuring the true logical form of sentences about how things look to people.

Now it is clear that Ayer, for example, does take sentences in the sense-datum language to be sentences in the full sense and to have logical relations of their own, relations which are not entirely parasitic on relations between sentences in the physical object language. He does not think that the meaning of sense-datum sentences is exhausted by stipulative definitions of the kind discussed so far. Nevertheless, he still holds that there is a sense in which his commitment to sense-data is not a factual commitment. But Sellars would see this as the result of confusion. Advocates of the alternative language thesis do not treat sense-datum 'sentences' as unstructured code symbols because they succumb to a constant temptation to treat sense-datum 'sentences' as though they really were

> . . . sentences in a theory, and a sense-datum talk as a *language* which gets its use by co-ordinating sense-datum sentences with sentences in ordinary perception talk, *as molecule talk gets its use by co-ordinating sentences about populations of molecules with talk about the pressure of gases on the walls of their containers.* [33]
>
> (Italics in original)

Misled by a superficial similarity, they confuse the sort of stipulations used to introduce the terminology of sense-data, which is supposed to be merely a piece of terminology, with the sort of postulates which give empirical meaning to theoretical terms.

Plausible as it is, I do not think that this gives a correct account of what is wrong with the alternative language thesis, at least as presented by Ayer. To begin with, although Sellars' account requires that the 'sentences' which come to be confused with genuine sentences in a theory be originally introduced as semantically unstructured code symbols, Ayer never shows the slightest tendency to think of the sentences in his sense-datum language as anything other than genuine sentences. That is, he thinks from the beginning that sense-datum talk really does offer an alternative *language* and not just an alternative (and misleading) set of symbols the meanings of which are exhaustively given by stipulative

[33] Sellars, op. cit., p. 138.

correlations with sentences taken from everyday talk about perception. To introduce such a range of symbols is not really to introduce a language at all: and we may add that, even if it were, the way in which the sentences of this language get their meanings would preclude its being in any interesting sense an *alternative*. Secondly, the temptation which Sellars sees lying in wait for the likes of Ayer involves confusing sense-datum 'sentences' with sentences in a theory. But to fall prey to this confusion would be to make an extraordinarily gross error since the main point of the alternative language account of sense-data is to distinguish between the introduction of a new language and the introduction of a new theory. What we want to know is how a philosopher might think it possible to draw the sharp distinction that the alternative language thesis requires.

I think that Ayer's claim that different philosophical theories of perception reflect advocacy of alternative languages becomes intelligible if we recall what I have called the 'two components view' of knowledge or experience. This is the view which, in Lewis's words, distinguishes '. . . in our cognitive experience, two elements; the immediate data such as those of sense, which are presented or given to the mind, and a form, construction, or interpretation, which represent the activity of thought.'[34] The data constitute the 'brute fact element' in experience, which Lewis calls 'the sensuous'.

As we saw, Lewis also expresses the distinction he has in mind by contrasting the sensuously given with the concept:

> . . . the two elements to be distinguished in knowledge are the concept, which is the product of the activity of thought, and the sensuously given, which is independent of such activity.[35]

This view of knowledge and experience is reflected in the

[34] Lewis, op. cit., p. 38.
[35] Ibid., p. 37.

alleged distinction between analysic and synthetic propositions. Analytic propositions are true in virtue of meaning, or by convention; synthetic propositions depend for
their truth on the way the world is.

Given a commitment to this way of thinking about
cognitive experience, it is easy to see how someone might
think it possible to adopt a totally different language—a
complete new system of concepts—without thereby being
committed to any disagreement about 'the facts'. After all,
given the same history in brute fact terms, we might still
disagree about the most convenient way of 'carving it up'.
Some of us might prefer a physical-object language on
account of its practical advantages. It does appear to be the
way of talking best adapted to the practical demands of
everyday life. But for special purposes, such as the
philosophical study of perceptual knowledge, another
terminology might be preferable, even though 'the facts' are
not in dispute.

Of course, if we reject the distinction between the given
and its interpretation or, which comes to the same thing, the
distinction between analytic truths which are explicative of
concepts and synthetic, factual truths, then we will have no
room for the distinction between the adoption of a new
language and the adoption of a new theory. But within the
traditional framework, there is plenty of room for such a
distinction.

When Ayer's position is explicated in these terms it is easy
to understand his disagreement with Carnap, a dispute which
can seem puzzling, given Ayer's own conventionalist
leanings. Carnap held that the question 'What objects are the
elements of given direct experience?' is merely verbal and
equivalent to asking 'What kinds of words occur in
observation sentences?' The answer depends wholly on one's
choice of language. Contrary to what one might have
expected, Ayer could not accept Carnap's view:

The choice of the language of sense-data to describe what we observe, rather than the language of appearing, or the language of multiple location, is indeed conventional; and it is a matter of convention that in referring to sense-data we should use the particular signs that we do. But it does not follow from this that the propositions which are intended to describe the characteristics of sense-data are true only by convention. For sense-data can have properties other than those that belong to them by definition; and to describe these properties is not to express a rule of language, but to make a statement of fact.[36]

Only some truths about sense-data are conventional, or analytic. Others depend on the facts. It is clear that Ayer is operating with a notion of observable fact such that there are observable facts knowledge of which does not depend on the possession of any particular system of concepts. These facts are in effect neutral with respect to all conceptual systems. Ayer echoes Lewis's distinction when he argues for the need to recognize two kinds of linguistic rule:

. . . it is necessary that, besides the rules which correlate symbols with other symbols, our language should also contain rules of meaning, which correlate symbols with observable facts.[37]

Ayer's commitment to a distinction between the given and its interpretation which is essentially the same as that argued for by Lewis explains both why he thinks that there can be different languages which do not reflect any disagreement about 'the facts' and also why he rejects Carnap's view that the decision about what is given is to be determined conventionally. Also, it should be clear by now just why

[36] Ayer, *Foundations*, pp. 113-14.
[37] Ibid., p. 112.

Sellars' account of the alternative language thesis is inadequate. The confusion Sellars attributes to alternative language theorists arises out of their thinking of sense-datum talk not as a mere notational device but as a 'language which gets its use by co-ordinating sense-datum sentences with sentences in ordinary perception talk.' However, the primitive terms of Ayer's sense-datum language will not ultimately derive their meanings from rules which 'correlate symbols with other symbols' but, as with any other language, from 'rules which correlate symbols with observable facts'. But merely to introduce a range of terms which describe such basic observational facts is not yet to commit oneself to any particular view of how these 'facts' arrange themselves, and this is why it is thought possible to adopt an alternative language without acquiring a commitment to an alternative theory. On the other hand, it should be equally clear that the 'facts' which Ayer takes to be neutral with respect to all conceptual systems are sense-datum facts. They must be, if only for the reason that, in Ayer's view, facts about physical objects can never be conclusively established by any finite stretch of anyone's experience and thus can never be ostensively given. But facts which can never be ostensively given cannot figure in those fundamental rules of meaning which 'correlate symbols with observable facts'.

If I am right, Ayer's suggestion that the sense-datum theory is simply an alternative language presupposes a prior commitment to the theory itself, or at the very least to the basic distinctions which make the theory plausible. Without these distinctions, Ayer's thesis is not even intelligible. It follows that the alternative language thesis does not help clarify the sense-datum theory or the appeal to the given which that theory embodies. It simply reflects that way of looking at cognitive experience. To put the point in the strongest terms, what his position comes to is this: if you are a phenomenalist, and believe that anything that can be said in a 'physical object' language can also be expressed using only the terminology of sense-data (since, after all, in the last analysis sense-datum facts are all the facts there are), then it is a matter of convention whether to adopt the physical object language or the language of sensa-data. But this shows graphically what is wrong with the alternative language thesis as an explication of phenomenalism: the thesis requires a prior commitment to phenomenalism itself.

This means that we cannot in the end take the alternative language thesis seriously. Adopting the framework of distinctions and assumptions which constitute the theoretical commitment of all phenomenalist theories is not a conventional matter. So the adoption of the sense-datum theory cannot be represented as evincing a preference for an alternative language. Only in the context of a prior commitment to phenomenalism can the suggestion that the adoption of the sense-datum language in preference to the language of physical objects reflects no disagreement about 'the facts' be seen to make any sense at all.

6. TWO APPROACHES TO THE GIVEN

The idea that the data of sensory experience are simply found by introspection was rejected earlier. We have also seen that Ayer's alternative language account of the appeal to the given leads nowhere. The conclusion to be drawn is that we must take seriously the idea that the framework of givenness has a theoretical role to play. We must ask just what that role is.

As we saw, Lewis argued that the distinction between the given and its interpretation is required for an understanding of the distinction between the true and the false. His interest here is epistemological. That is, he is not presupposing that a sharp distinction be drawn between 'the theory of truth' and 'the theory of evidence'. He is looking for the same thing as Price: an ultimate base of non-inferential knowledge against which all other claims can be checked.

Chisholm argues that this idea—that empirical knowledge rests, indeed must rest, on a foundation of non-inferential knowledge, some of which at least is observational knowledge—is the fundamental insight captured by the notion that there is a given element in experience.[38] If correct, this could appear to draw the sting from many criticisms which might be levelled at the framework of givenness. Perhaps we can dispense with the unhappy connexion between givenness and non-propositional knowledge. All the theory requires is that there be a foundation of observational knowledge expressible in a theory-neutral observation language: there is no need to postulate a level at which knowledge becomes non-propositional. Perhaps, too, we can avoid worrying about whether most of our knowledge-claims have to be the products of actual processes of inference. The 'immediacy' of ordinary perceptual consciousness has been a powerful source of disenchantment with the idea that we are 'given' only phenomenal qualities and have to infer the existence of physical objects: but if the theory is concerned with the logical structure of empirical knowledge rather than with its genesis, it may be that such worries are misplaced. I shall argue that it is not so easy to escape the difficulties which arise in an attempt to think through traditional versions of the appeal to the given. The appeal to givenness in its strongest form arises out of the attempt to explicate the idea that knowledge rests on a foundation, the attempt to show how foundational knowledge is possible.

Chisholm claims that the doctrine of the given involves two main theses about knowledge, both of which he takes to be true. These are as follows:

---

[38] R. M. Chisholm in *Humanistic Scholarship in America, The Princeton Studies: Philosophy* (Englewood Cliffs, N.J.: Prentice-Hall, 1964). Chisholm contributes the article on the theory of knowledge. See especially section 2, 'The Myth of the Given'.

(A)   The knowledge which a person has at any time is a structure or edifice, many parts and stages of which help to support each other, but which as a whole is supported by its own foundation.

(B)   The foundation of one's knowledge consists (at least in part) of the apprehension of what have been called, variously, 'sensations', 'sense-impressions', 'appearances', 'sensa', 'sense-qualia', and 'phenomena'.[39]

This is just the view we found to be presupposed by Ayer's formulation of the argument for radical scepticism. We are led to it, Chisholm thinks, by an attempt to answer certain questions about justification.

The trouble with the claim that the doctrine of the given involves both (A) and (B) is that this account identifies the doctrine with the sense-datum theory. This is historically inaccurate since the question 'What kinds of things are given?' has occasioned much controversy. Worse, we may be tempted into thinking that a critique of the sense-datum theory is a critique of givenness per se. A better course is to take the essence of the doctrine to be given by (A). We can then agree that the sense-datum theory is perhaps the most important version, but still recognize that other versions are possible and have been held.[40]

Some of these alternative versions of the theory may reasonably be assimilated to the sense-datum theory. For example, Firth has defended a position he calls 'the Percept Theory' according to which 'ostensible physical objects' rather than sense-data, conceived as Price's coloured patches, are given.[41] But these 'ostensible physical objects',

---

[39] Ibid., p. 261.

[40] For a useful survey of various theories of the given see J. J. Ross, *The Appeal to the Given* (London: Allen and Unwin, 1970).

[41] Roderick Firth, 'Sense-Data and the Percept Theory', *Mind*, Vol. LVIII (1949) Pt. 1, and Vol. LIX (1950), p. 2, Reprinted in Swartz, p. cit.

since not identical with physical objects proper, are to all intents and purposes sense-data, though of a phenomenologically rich variety.

But what about direct realism? I suggested earlier that even this position can be associated with the doctrine of the given. The availability of this option shows that (A) and (B) can fall apart. For a direct realist can hold that certain kinds of perceptual beliefs about physical objects are epistemologically basic, thus holding to (A), while denying this status to beliefs about sense-date or the like. Such a view could result from a disposition to be sympathetic both towards the foundational picture of knowledge and towards some form of behaviourism as a way of dealing with the epistemological problems arising out of the privacy of mental events, such as the having of sensations.

I think, then, that Chisholm is right to identify the claim that empirical knowledge must rest on a foundation of non-inferential knowledge, some of which at least is observational knowledge, as the fundamental idea behind the notion that there is a given element in experience. But I also think that to identify this foundational knowledge with the apprehension of 'sensations', 'appearances' and so on is to take a further step. Since Chisholm's (A) and (B) are not necessarily connected, there arises the question of why they should be thought to be so closely linked. However, this is a question best answered after we have come to grips with the reasons for thinking that empirical knowledge must have some kind of foundational structure and, hopefully, made more apparent just what that idea involves. To this task I now turn.

3. The Regress of Justification

1. INTRODUCTORY REMARKS

I suggested in chapter two that the main idea behind phenomenalism is that there are epistemologically basic beliefs which are in some way perceptual beliefs and which serve as a foundation—or at least a partial foundation—for our beliefs about the physical world. It is quite widely believed that certain considerations compel us to adopt a theory of perceptual knowledge which is phenomenalistic in my wide sense. I shall argue that they fail in this. However, by following through the arguments for epistemologically basic, or foundational beliefs, we shall be able to shed some light on what it is for a belief to fulfil a foundational role, a notion so far left obscure. Thus armed, I shall try to see whether a phenomenalist theory can be developed in a plausible way. I shall argue that any such theory faces intolerable difficulties. Since the arguments first examined are less than compelling, we shall be justified in rejecting all forms of phenomenalism and the foundational view of knowledge on which they depend.

2. BASIC BELIEFS

The phenomenalist sees knowledge as having a foundational structure with perceptual beliefs at the bottom. It would be possible to hold a foundational theory which based knowledge on beliefs of some other kind. But perceptual beliefs of some sort look to be the most plausible candidates. Since perception seems to provide the link between the knowing mind and the world at large, beliefs having something to do with perception should find a special place in the scheme of things. Phenomenalism, as I see it, comes to the same thing as Chisholm's reconstructed doctrine of the given, mentioned in chapter two.

Let us, provisionally, define epistemologically basic beliefs to be beliefs on the basis of which other beliefs are justified but which do not themselves require justification. We can say that such beliefs are *intrinsically credible.* The point of epistemologically basic beliefs is that they provide ultimate terminating points for chains of justification.

If the basic beliefs are really to constitute a foundation, not all inferential moves from basic to non-basic beliefs can be allowed to depend on background knowledge. This brings us to another theme, central to orthodox phenomenalist theories: that at least some epistemic relations between basic and non-basic beliefs must be such that they can be known to hold a priori. This point is sometimes expressed by saying that basic beliefs must in some instances constitute logical and not merely contingent reasons for the higher-level beliefs they justify. The idea that such evidential connexions hold in virtue of meaning, that there is some kind of analytic connexion between basic and non-basic beliefs, offers the most popular and most plausible account of how this is possible.

To say that these connexions are analytic implies that they hold in virtue of meaning and independently of fact. They are thus safe from revision. If we were to abandon such a connexion, we should have changed the meanings of some of our terms, but we should not have denied a previously accepted fact about the world.

Must the intrinsically credible basic beliefs be safe from revision in the light of experience? Many philosophers who have wanted to base knowledge on a fund of absolutely certain beliefs have obviously thought so. But, on the face of things, there is no reason to accept this view. Epistemologically basic beliefs provide ultimate terminating points for chains of justification, but this seems at most to imply that these beliefs must be such that one can be *justified* in holding them without being able to supply independent justification. Nothing has been said to incline us to the view that such beliefs enjoy absolute safety. They may be prima-facie justified, but defeasible.

Whether we opt for incorrigibility or only prima-facie justification, the credibility of the basic beliefs must still be intrinsic. That is, their justification must not accrue to them through knowledge of any general facts about the world, or any further background knowledge. This is implied by their being ultimate terminating points for chains of justification. So to say that a basic belief is prima-facie justified is to say more than that it is a belief that we can see no particular need to question right now, given our other beliefs. It is to say that there is a logical presumption in favour of the belief's being true, though not a guarantee. The cash-value of the notion of a logical presumption in favour of a belief's being true seems to be this: that it is analytically true that, in holding beliefs of that kind, we are right most of the time. However, for reasons that will emerge later, I do not think that much turns on the question of whether or not the intrinsic credibility attaching to epistemologically basic beliefs adds up to strict incorrigibility.

3. The Regress Argument

Not every case of true belief is a case of knowledge. This has led philosophers to ask what must be added to true belief to give knowledge. The traditional answer, which I am accepting, is that one's belief must be not only true but also justified. But there is also a traditional difficulty. To say that one is justified in believing that P is to say that one has good reasons for believing that P: that is, there must be some other things counting in favour of P that one knows, that one is justified in believing. This presupposes the possession of yet further justified beliefs, and so on. We seem to have landed ourselves in an infinite regress of justification.

By 'an infinite regress of justification' I would be understood to mean either an infinite linear chain or a circular chain of justification. For it is conceivable that following through the justification for a given belief might eventually lead us back to that belief itself.

Consideration of the threat of the regress of justification can lead straight to the postulation of epistemologically basic beliefs, beliefs that are *intrinsically* credible. The idea is that the threat of the regress forces us to recognize that not all knowledge can be inferential in the sense of based on further justified beliefs. To escape the regress we must admit the existence of beliefs that can be justified without their justification accruing to them from further beliefs. In other words, we must recognize the existence of beliefs which are intrinsically credible. If we agree that perception is an important source of knowledge about the physical world, we shall be prepared to admit that at least some of our basic beliefs must have something to do with perception. This leads us to a theory of knowledge which is, in my broad sense, phenomenalistic.

This line of thought, and variations upon it, provide the main impetus towards the foundational view of knowledge central to all phenomenalistic theories. It is manifested in the principle adopted by C. I. Lewis and Norman Malcolm to the effect that unless some things are certain, nothing else is even probable.[1] It is all very well to know that a particular

[1] C. I. Lewis, 'The Given Element in Empirical Knowledge', a contribution to a symposium with Hans Reichenbach and Nelson

statement is probable with respect to certain premises: but what about the premises themselves? If we say that these premises are themselves merely probable, this will mean that they are probable with respect to some further premises, and so on without end. Without end, that is, unless there are some beliefs whose credibility is intrinsic.

Price's attempt to discover the given element in experience by seeing what he could doubt when he looked at a tomato also turns out to be underpinned by the regress argument. He writes:

> . . . the data of the historian are the statements which he finds in documents and inscriptions; the data of the general are the facts reported by his aircraft and his intelligence service; the data of the detective are the known circumstances and known results of the crime; and so on. But it is obvious that these are only data relatively and for the purpose of answering a certain question. They are really themselves the results of inference, often of a very complicated kind. We may call them data *secundum quid.* But eventually we must get back to something which is a datum *simpliciter,* which is not the result of any previous intellectual process.[2]

Price's acceptance of the regress argument gives us an insight into why he thought that the philosophical study of perception had to proceed on the basis of pure inspection. To bring into play scientific facts about perception would be to appeal to beliefs belonging to a higher level of complexity, in

Goodman in *The Philosophical Review*, Vol. 61, 2 (April 1952), pp. 168-173. Both Reichenbach and Goodman are critical of Lewis's position. A similar principle is implicit in Malcolm's discussion of our knowledge of other minds and the argument from analogy. See e.g. 'Knowledge of Other Minds', in Malcolm, *Knowledge and Certainty* (Englewood Cliffs, N.J.: Prentice-Hall, 1963).

[2] Price, op. cit., p. 4.

fact some of the very beliefs whose perceptual underpinnings the philosopher is concerned to find; and this would be circular.

Price noticed a consequence of this which other phenomenalists have not always heeded. This is that phenomenalism looks to be incompatible with a thoroughgoing scientific approach to the world. Price did not put the point in quite these terms, but his remarks clearly point in this direction. His view is that

> Empirical Science can never be more trustworthy than perception, upon which it is based; and it can hardly fail to be *less* so, since among its non-perceptual premises there can hardly fail to be some which are neither self-evident nor demonstrable. Thus the not uncommon view that the world which we perceive is an illusion and only the 'scientific' world of protons and electrons is real, is based upon a gross fallacy, and would destroy the very premises upon which Science itself depends.[3]

Thus the study of the various modes of sense-perception 'lies outside the sphere of science altogether'.[4]

That phenomenalism should be incompatible with a thoroughgoing scientific realism is not surprising. For if any phenomenalistic theory is correct—that is, if any theory which recognizes the existence of epistemologically basic beliefs is correct— then there exists a class of beliefs whose general credibility cannot be impugned, however much we may come to change our scientific views about the world. This is so whether we take the basic beliefs to be incorrigible or whether we merely take them to be such that there is a logical presumption in favour of a basic belief's being true, for the notion of a logical presumption was explicated in terms of conceptual—hence necessary—truth. This provides

[3] Ibid., p. 1.
[4] Ibid., p. 2.

further justification for my taking all epistemological theories which require the existence of epistemologically basic perceptual beliefs to be of a piece (and grouping them under the rubric 'phenomenalism'). For it now appears that there is a genuine alternative to all of them: that is, a thoroughgoing scientific realism which takes empirical inquiry and not epistemological necessity, or phenomenological inspection, to be the ultimate measure of what there is.

Price's remarks do not merely raise the question of whether a phenomenalist theory of knowledge is compatible with a consistently scientific outlook. They also point to a particular difficulty for phenomenalist theories. This problem is: how do we know that alleged data are really *data*? In our terminology, how can we show that statements of a given type really are *intrinsically* credible? We cannot appeal to any empirically established facts about the world for to do so would be to fall foul of the regress of justification. With admirable consistency, Price is driven to appeal to a kind of pure phenomenological inspection, a procedure which lies outside the scope of science. But this strikes me as a reductio ad absurdum of the whole enterprise. Seeing and touching form the main basis of empirical knowledge. To discover what they themselves are, the question which Price takes to lie outside the scope of science, each of us is supposed to take an unbiased introspective look at his perceptual data. We are supposed just to *see* that such data exist and really are *data*. The object of our introspective investigation is whatever is *directly* given to consciousness: as Price puts it, 'our consciousness of it is not reached by inference, nor by any other intellectual process (such as abstraction or intuitive induction)'. This latter condition seems to exclude even describing what we find with the aid of general terms (this would involve 'abstraction'). Not surprisingly, it turns out that 'sensuousness', the internal characteristic which distinguishes sense-data from other kinds of data, memory-data for example, is said to be 'obvious on inspection, but it cannot be described'. The study of seeing and touching *themselves* turns out to be a solitary search for ineffable conclusions.

At this point, someone might be inclined to object that there is really no problem here and that the whole regress argument is specious. Surely, it could be said, the threat of the regress arises only because of an assumption that basic beliefs (taken by the objector to be merely beliefs for which we can state no justification but which can nevertheless constitute knowledge) must not simply be reliable, but that the person who entertains the beliefs must know something at least about *why* they can be relied on. But if this latter condition is removed—if we do not insist that a person be able to justify his reliance on his basic beliefs—the regress disappears. This proposal is in the spirit of those analyses of knowledge, briefly discussed in chapter one, which equate knowledge with belief reached by a reliable method.

Such a proposal cuts the ground from under the argument for intrinsically credible beliefs, or seems to. For if the regress can be blocked this way, we can give an account of basic knowledge in terms of belief the occurrence of which is *empirically* sufficient for its being true (if we wish to argue for incorrigibility), or at least justified (if we do not).[5] Consider, for example, the special epistemic status and non-inferential character of observation statements, like 'There is something red in front of me'. Following Sellars, we could say that a person's utterances of sentences like 'There is something red in front of me' can be said to express observational knowledge because they are manifestations of a tendency, given the appropriate disposition towards reporting his observations, to make such utterances when and only when he is in the sensory state normally brought

[5] Something along these lines is defended by D. M. Armstrong in *A Materialist Theory of the Mind* (London: Routledge, Kegan Paul, 1968), ch. 9. Armstrong's concerns are, however, rather different from my own.

about by stimulation from red objects.[6] The important point Sellars makes is that, in order to explain how it is possible for us to make credible yet non-inferential reports, we do not need to appeal to prelinguistic awareness of basic 'phenomenal' qualities, but can look instead to the fact that human beings can be trained to respond directly and reliably to certain stimulus conditions. This means, in effect, that our immediate perceptual beliefs, when true, can constitute knowledge in virtue of the fact that our coming to hold such a belief is empirically sufficient for its being justified and this, in turn, is simply because, as a matter of fact, there are many features of our environment of which we are generally reliable observers.

Sellars does not think that for a person to be capable of expressing observational knowledge it is sufficient that he be in possession of the right linguistic habits. After all, a parrot could satisfy that condition. Rather he holds that for a report to be an expression of knowledge it must not simply be credible: its credibility must also be recognized by the person whose report it is. In particular, the perceiver must know that tokens of 'This is green' are symptoms for the presence of green objects in conditions which are standard for visual perception. Sellars realizes that this raises the threat of a regress. How could we have acquired knowledge of such general facts unless we had had prior observational knowledge of certain particular facts, and if this presupposes further knowledge of general facts . . .

We have seen that intuitions can differ as to how much we have to know about the justification for our beliefs in order for them to count as knowledge. Some philosophers do not find it at all counter-intuitive to equate knowledge with belief reached by a reliable method. They do not insist that the method itself be an object of knowledge. Even so, I do not think that we have yet found a final way out of the regress

---

[6] Sellars, op. cit., pp. 166-168.

argument. Suppose that the justification for our relying on perceptual beliefs in the way that we do were to be empirically grounded—grounded in facts about human perceivers, their learning capabilities and so on—but we just didn't happen to know about it: then empirical knowledge would have a 'foundation' only until we found out what the grounds for the credibility of our 'basic' beliefs were. Since these would be formulated in non-basic terms, scientific progress would have made us vulnerable to the regress argument. Any foundational theorist must find such a possibility intolerable. What this shows is that, if a defender of phenomenalism is to have an argument for intrinsically credible beliefs (epistemologically basic beliefs in the strong sense), he must object to there being even a potential infinite regress of justification. Surely this is what was meant all along. For phenomenalism is not just concerned with what any particular person, or all of us for that matter, might happen to know at some time: the theory concerns the *structure* of justification, what the grounds for certain beliefs *are,* and not just whether anyone happens to be aware of them.

An important point which emerges from this is that the sense in which Sellars' account of observation-reports allows such reports to be non-inferential is very different from that required by a foundational theory. Sellars equates being able to report non-inferentially with being able to report 'without thinking about it'. In this (quite untechnical) sense of 'non-inferential', there is no a priori limit to the kinds of things upon which, given proper training, we could come to report non-inferentially. But when a defender of phenomenalism argues that empirical knowledge at large rests on a foundation of non-inferential perceptual knowledge, he has a much stronger sense of 'non-inferential' in mind. For if we are to rule out the possibility of even a potential regress of justification, basic perceptual reports must not merely be such that we can make them reliably on cue and hence, in general, have them accepted at face-value: rather they must be such that, in the nature of the case, no further justification is either required or possible. As I put it, they must be intrinsically credible. The range of statements possessing this property—often called that of being 'directly knowable'—has generally been thought to be fixed in advance. And there is a certain appeal to this view, since it promises a permanent body of observational knowledge, independent of all theory, against which any theory is to be tested. Sellars' account of non-inferential perceptual reports does not guarantee them the status of being directly knowable, because it makes the general credibility of such reports depend on contingent (and certainly not theory-free) facts about the perceptual and linguistic abilities of human beings. Our having the ability to make non-inferential reports, in the sense of reports which, though credible, are not based on any actual process of inference, is compatible with nothing that we know being non-inferential in the sense demanded by a phenomenalistic theory of knowledge.

A consequence of this is that we should distinguish two kinds of direct realism. If we take direct realism to be the thesis that certain facts about physical objects are non-inferentially knowable, direct realism may or may not involve a commitment to the existence of foundational knowledge. It will involve such a commitment if we understand 'non-inferentially knowable' to be equivalent to 'intrinsically credible'. Direct realism, thus construed, accepts a foundational view of knowledge, but sets the foundations at the level of perceptual reports of certain facts about physical objects. This seems to be what Ayer has in mind when he talks about 'naive' realism. But if we explicate the capacity for having non-inferential knowledge of Xs in terms of having the ability to make reliable, off-the-cuff reports on certain facts about Xs—and this is the account of non-inferential knowledge suggested by the idea that the credibility of observation reports is to be traced to the abilities human beings have to respond directly to some things, though not to others—then no commitment to foundationalism is involved. On the contrary, the whole point of such theories of observational knowledge is to be anti-foundationalist.

An account of observational knowledge along the lines suggested by Sellars in no way favours the view that we can report 'immediately' only on the contents of 'immediate experience'. The opposite is true. Once we explain the credibility and non-inferential character of observation reports in this manner, there is no need to abandon the commonsense idea that the reports we make on the perceptible qualities of physical objects are paradigm expressions of observational knowledge. So if we can defend empirical accounts of the credibility attaching to non-inferential observation reports against the foundationalist charge that such theories involve us in a vicious infinite regress of justification, there will be a sense in which, by rejecting foundationalism, we shall have offered a defence of direct realism.

4. SETTING THE FOUNDATIONS

This is a good point at which to pick up a question left hanging at the end of chapter two. Chisholm, we may recall, claims that the idea that there is a given element in experience breaks down into two theses: that empirical knowledge rests on a foundation, at least part of which is observational, and that this basic observational knowledge concerns 'sensations', 'appearances', 'sense-data' or 'qualia'. We saw that these two claims can be separated and were thus faced with the question of why they might be thought to be so closely connected.

Chisholm's account of the doctrine of the given identifies it with the sense-datum theory, a theory which Sellars has argued results from the crossbreeding of two ideas:

(1)   The idea that there are certain inner episodes—e.g. sensations of red or of C♯ which can occur to human beings (and brutes) without any prior process of learning or concept formation; and without which it would *in some sense* be impossible to see, for example, that the facing surface of a physical object is red and triangular, or *hear* that a certain sound is C♯.

(2)   The idea that there are certain inner episodes which are the non-inferential knowings that certain items are, for example, red or C♯; and that these episodes are the necessary conditions of empirical knowledge, as providing the evidence for all other empirical propositions.[7]

(2) is just another way of stating the idea that empirical knowledge rests on its proper foundations. (1), on the other hand, arises in the course of an attempt to give something like a scientific account of the facts of perceptual experience. The phenomena of hallucinatory perception, seeing double, seeing objects through various distorting media, consideration of which has often been argued to lead to the conclusion that only sense-data are directly perceived, do seem to raise a real question: how is it that one can have an experience which one might describe by saying it is as though one were seeing a red apple when there is no object of that type, perhaps even no object at all, there to be seen? A plausible answer is that anyone who has such an experience has a 'sensation' or 'impression' of a red apple. In a normal adult, having such a sensation will generally lead to a disposition to believe that he is seeing a red apple. However, such states of the perceiver need not necessarily be brought about by red apples affecting his sensory apparatus, although in 'normal circumstances' they will be.

The important point to notice about this explanation is that it gives no reason to think of the having of a sensation as

[7] Ibid., p. 132.

a cognitive or epistemic fact. In an epistemological context, the force of 'immediate' is 'without inference' and the move from the immediately perceived to the mediately perceived is inferential and epistemic. Now the theory introduced in connection with perceptual relativity, hallucination, and so on, does involve the claim that our knowledge of the physical world is, in a sense, mediated by the having of sensations, but it is a further step to insist that *this* mediation is epistemic rather than merely causal. Thus the fact, if it is a fact, that our perceptual beliefs are mediated by the having of sensations need not prevent such beliefs from constituting, on occasion, direct or non-inferential knowledge of the physical world. However, it is easy to run these two lines of thought together, particularly if one is in search of absolutely certain foundations for empirical knowledge and has become overly impressed with the fact that 'sensations' cannot be said to be 'non-veridical'. The result is the idea that the foundations of empirical knowledge are to be set at the level of sensations.

There is a lot to be said for this account of the sense-datum theory. For one thing, it helps us understand why there might be a puzzle about the theoretical status of sensations or sense-data. If these are supposed to be the objects of basic non-inferential knowledge, an air of contradiction clings to the suggestion that they are in any way theoretical entities: their being such would seem to conflict with their being given. But there is nothing obviously absurd about the idea that sensations are theoretical when they are seen as entities postulated in the course of trying to give an account of various perceptual phenomena. It is clear that Price was confused on just this issue, which is why he was led to advocate pure inspection, a method which lies quite outside science, as the proper method for the study of perception. If his aim was to give a scientific theory of perception, he could have appealed to whatever scientific hypotheses and procedures suited his purpose; but if his aim was to account for the credibility of epistemologically basic beliefs, then to have appealed to knowledge belonging to a higher level in the epistemological order would have been to fall foul of the regress of justification and to abandon the idea that empirical knowledge rests on its proper foundations.

Still, I do not think that this is the whole story. Even if many phenomenalists have confused the non-cognitive having of sensations with the acquisition of non-inferential perceptual knowledge, this does not look like a mistake they are compelled to make. A phenomenalist could talk consistently about *beliefs about* how one is appeared to and claim that these beliefs, not the sensations themselves, lie at the foundations. Many modern phenomenalists do talk this way. But if they do not fall into the trap described by Sellars, do they have any reason to locate the foundations at the level of beliefs about how one is appeared to rather than at the level of beliefs about the perceptible qualities of objects in the physical world?

How is it that sensations have so often been thought to lie at the basis of empirical knowledge? Philosophers most likely to cast sensations for this role are those who hold that foundational beliefs must actually be incorrigible: it is obvious that beliefs about the perceptible qualities of physical objects do not live up to such a requirement. This is where the various phenomena of aberrant perception play an important epistemological role. Beliefs about the observable characteristics of physical objects cannot be incorrigible and hence, it is argued, cannot be epistemologically basic, because one can seem to see an object with such and such properties without actually doing so, and this experience of 'seeming to see', at least within the confines of a 'single perceptual act', may be indistinguishable from the 'veridical' experience of perceiving the object as it really is. There need be no intrinsic features by means of which non-veridical experiences may be identified and, in the light of our discussion in the previous section, we may add that it would not matter much if there were. After all, if there were such an indicator of non-veridical experiences, it would presumably have to have been established empirically that experiences of such and such a character were invariably non-veridical, in which case the process of identifying non-veridical experiences by this phenomenal feature would call implicitly on prior knowledge of general facts, as well as on some independent and non-immediate criterion of non-veridicality, and so would yield inferential rather than immediate knowledge. These reflections should also make clear that arguments intended to show that we do not have direct knowledge of facts about physical objects do not count in favour of a foundational view of knowledge. Rather, if such arguments show anything at all, they show, given that there must be foundations, that these cannot be set at the level of knowledge of the physical world. The fact that we cannot tell within the space of a single perceptual act which of our experiences are veridical is supposed to show that beliefs about physical objects cannot be intrinsically credible, but this conclusion is of no significance unless it is assumed in advance that intrinsic credibility must be somewhere to be found.

Sensations can seem attractive candidates for the role of purveyors of non-inferential knowledge but, as we saw in chapter two, the sense in which sensations cannot be non-veridical is of no epistemological significance. If having a sensation is not an episode of 'knowing that', the having of sensations cannot constitute the foundations of empirical knowledge. Nevertheless, to come to the main point, it is worth emphasizing that even if a phenomenalist does not confuse the non-cognitive having of sensations with the acquisition of non-inferential knowledge and talks instead in terms of beliefs about, say, how one is appeared to, he will still be under pressure to set the foundations of knowledge at this level rather than at the level of beliefs about physical objects if he continues to think that the intrinsically credible basic beliefs must be strictly incorrigible. Beliefs about the observable characteristics of physical objects are obviously not incorrigible and, if incorrigible foundations are demanded, there is at least a chance of making out a case for the incorrigible status of more guarded claims about how one is appeared to, though whether the case can really be made out is another question.

A proponent of the foundational view of knowledge can resist setting the foundations at the level of appearances if he holds that the foundational beliefs need only be prima-facie justified, hence defeasible. Of course, he must still hold that they are intrinsically credible. I suggested earlier that this intrinsic prima-facie justification could be explicated in terms of there being a logical presumption in favour of beliefs of a certain kind being true. Our consideration of the regress argument shows that this is the only way to explicate it, for we saw that to say that there is an *empirical* presumption in favour of beliefs of a certain kind being true is to trace the prima-facie credibility of these beliefs to further general facts and thus to lead ourselves back into the very regress from which *intrinsically* credible beliefs are supposed to liberate us. Thus an appeal to an empirical presumption will not give an account of intrinsic prima-facie credibility: we must have recourse to the notion of a logical presumption. A phenomenalist who does not find this account of intrinsic credibility plausible will have to set the foundations of knowledge at the level of appearances.

Since the foundations can be set at the level of beliefs involving corrigible physical object statements only if we are prepared to countenance the notion of a logical presumption in favour of a belief's being true, and since I reject the concept of analytic or conceptual truth, on which the notion of a logical presumption depends, I cannot look favourably on the idea that the foundational view might be made more palatable by resisting the temptation to set the foundations at the level of sense-data or appearances. But even if I were to accept that some truths could plausibly be regarded as analytic, I should not look much more favourably on this idea, for in the absence of a prior commitment to the foundational view, there is no reason at all to think that the presumption in favour of certain kinds of perceptual beliefs being true reflects some general conceptual, rather than empirical, truth.

5. LINGUISTIC RULES

Many philosophers influenced by Wittgenstein have thought that knowledge is a matter of the correct application of words, where the notion of correctness is explicated in terms of application in accordance with a particular kind of linguistic rule. Consideration of this notion of a linguistic rule offers another way into the regress and, consequently, points toward the apparent need to recognize the existence of epistemologically basic beliefs.

The Wittgensteinian concept of a linguistic rule is not without its problems. A natural explicatory move is to relate the notion of a rule to the notion of a criterion. The idea is that knowing how to apply a classificatory word—the state of having mastered a linguistic rule—is a matter of having mastered the criteria which govern its use. Suppose I want to know whether the thing on my plate is a tomato: I need to determine its colour, shape, internal makeup and so on. Presumably, some of these features at least are what Wittgenstein would call criteria for something's being a tomato. Stating the criteria for something's being a tomato is not necessarily a matter of giving the truth-conditions for the sentence 'That's a tomato.' Correct application is not always true application. An application of a word may be correct in the sense of being justified. Thus mastering the criteria for the application of a word is a matter of acquiring the ability to make justified assertions involving that word.

It has been claimed that this insight—that meaning is determined not just by truth-conditions, but also by justification conditions—enables us to see just what was wrong with 'reductionist' theories such as classical phenomenalism. Advocates of such theories realized the need to recognize non-inductive evidential connexions between, say, statements about physical objects and perceptual statements which provide the evidence for these. But because they thought that meaning was determined solely by truth-conditions, they thought that a meaning-link between statements in the problematic class and statements in the evidential class could be demonstrated only if members of the former could be 'analysed' in terms of members of the latter. The project failed. However, we will not be worried by this once we realize that, since meaning is also determined by justification-conditions, there can be relations of justification which hold in virtue of meaning. So the argument goes.[8]

The connexion between rules and criteria, then, is that in order to decide whether something is a tomato, or can correctly be called a tomato, one must have mastered the rules which specify the criteria for being a tomato. The important feature of such rules is that they serve to licence *inferences*. The rules which specify the criteria for being a tomato are rules which entitle us to infer that the thing on my plate is a tomato on the basis of having established that it has such and such a colour, shape, and so on. But how are these claims to be established? With the aid of criteria? This answer will only raise the same problem at one remove. The idea that the ability to make warranted assertions depends on having mastered rules which specify criteria for the classificatory words involved threatens us with an infinite regress, for it suggests that, in order to know that a given

---

[8] See John L. Pollock, 'What is an Epistemological Problem?' *American Philosophical Quarterly* (1968), pp. 183-190.

assertion is warranted, one has to know that some further claim is also warranted—i.e. the claim which records the fulfilment of the relevant 'criteria'. How is it possible for any claim ever to be justified? Pursuing this line of thought tends to lead inevitably to the idea that there must be some things, at least, which can be known without criteria, which is interpreted to mean that there must be some claims whose credibility is intrinsic. Given a basis of intrinsically credible beliefs, rules of inference which specify criteria permit the construction of a system of justified beliefs about the world.

Because the notion of a criterion figures prominently in explication of Wittgenstein's 'private language argument' —an argument which seem> designed to cut the ground out from under traditional phenomenalist theories of knowledge—one might think that philosophers who make a lot out of criteria are automatically hostile to the picture of justification which lies at the heart of such theories. But the preceding argument shows that this need not be so. Many 'Wittgensteinian' attacks on phenomenalism are not attacks on the notions I consider central to phenomenalist theories. At best, they are attacks on some fairly traditional conception of sense-data.

To pick up the main theme of this section, the regress is supposed to be blocked by appealing to a class of basic predicates applicable without criteria. But this might seem to raise as many problems as it solves. Originally, the idea of learning the correct use of a term was explained in terms of mastering the rules which specify the criteria for the use of that term. How, then, could one ever learn the correct use of a term applicable without criteria? This is the point at which a certain view of the nature of meaning, and its associated picture of language acquisition, are likely to suggest themselves. The idea is that the primitive predicates of our language are given their meaning, and consequently are learned, ostensively.

The appeal to ostension is worthless. Firstly, ostension is

itself an act whose meaning is no more obvious than that of any linguistic expression. Secondly, and more importantly, mere pointing is never sufficient to pick anything out. To understand what is being ostended, we need to understand some principles of classification. Suppose I point in the general direction of a red box: there will be no purely ostensive way for me to indicate that it is the shape rather than the colour, or even the box itself, that I intend to pick out. Consequently, the genesis of meaning cannot be sought in ostension since ostension can work only within an ongoing language which already contains principles of classification not established ostensively.

The force of this criticism will be missed by anyone gripped by the traditional framework of givenness. According to this theory, there are certain qualities, generally phenomenal qualities, of which we have prelinguistic awareness. So on this view there is a sense in which we do have a grasp of some relevant principles of classification, and this is what makes it possible to grasp the meaning of basic predicates through ostension. In this empiricist picture, catching on to the meaning of some primitive linguistic expression is like learning a name for something one has known all along.

Similar problems arise if we pursue the non-genetic question of the source of the credibility of the basic beliefs. If justification is to be related to correct usage, and correctness of usage to following rules, how can there be empirical claims whose credibility is intrinsic? For the linguistic rules which specify criteria governing correct use turned out to be rules of inference.

The natural move seems to be to recognize another kind of rule. The need to do this has been felt by philosophers before criteria came into vogue. In chapter two we noted Ayer's view that

. . . it is necessary that, besides the rules which correlate symbols with other symbols, our language should also contain rules of meaning, which correlate symbols with observable facts.[9]

This seems to be just what is needed in the present context. A basic statement turns out to be like an analytic statement in that its being correctly made, uttered in accordance with the rules, ensures its truth. But, as we saw, this kind of rule commits one to accepting the idea that there is a kind of knowledge of fact which is prior to, independent of, and indeed underpins all linguistic expression of thought. At the basic level, following the rules involves taking in the 'observable facts' and 'correlating' one's symbols with them. In other words, acceptance of this kind of linguistic rule brings with it acceptance of the doctrine of the given in its strongest form. We saw in chapter two just how much is wrong with that.

Someone might object at this point that we are taking a very roundabout approach to the problem. Surely this whole criteriological view of the nature of justification is wrong because it embodies an untenable conception of inference. The proponent of criteria holds that a justified system of beliefs about the world is held together by rules of the following general form:—If you can justifiably accept E then you should accept H also. But rules of this form could not be generally valid. Inference is often as much a matter of abandoning old beliefs as acquiring new ones. That is, H may be so implausible, *given one's further beliefs,* that it would be more rational to revoke one's initial acceptance of E, or to formulate some explanation as to why E does not in these circumstances provide a good reason for accepting H, than to go on to accept H on the basis of E. The point is that any change of belief through inference involves a good deal more of one's total belief system than the proponent of

---

[9] Ayer, *Foundations of Empirical Knowledge*, p. 112.

criteria seems to allow. (Perhaps all one's beliefs are involved.)[10]

I am very much in sympathy with this point, but it does not obviate the need to inquire whether there could be, or must be, such things as epistemologically basic beliefs. Even if inference does have a more holistic character than a naive criteriological theory would allow, it is still a further question whether certain beliefs function in a special way in the structure of justification. Even the most traditional phenomenalists, although they certainly recognized the existence of epistemologically basic beliefs—sense-datum beliefs, in their case—did not hold that every such belief constituted in itself grounds for an inference to a belief in the existence of a real object. Rather, constructing one's inferential picture of the physical world was held to be a matter of fitting as many as possible of one's sense-datum beliefs into a coherent overall account. Any sense-datum beliefs which could not be accommodated would have to be rejected as delusive. But to reject a sense-datum belief as delusive did not mean to reject it as false in itself, but only to reject it as an experience of the real.

Also, although proponents of criteria have sometimes claimed that criteria establish beyond question the existence of that for which they are criteria,[11] this is not the most careful formulation of the view. Advocates of the criteriological approach can allow that the rules of inference specifying criteria contain a ceteris paribus clause: but they do think that it is a necessary truth that criteria are *reliable* indicators, that exceptions to the rule are *necessarily* exceptions.

---

[10] A powerful critique of much philosophical thinking about inference has been developed by Gilbert Harman. For a recent statement of his views see his book *Thought*.

[11] E.g. by Norman Malcolm in his 'Review of Wittgenstein's 'Philosophical Investigations' ", *Philosophical Review*, 63 (1954), pp. 530-559. I do not mean to suggest that any of the views criticized in this section were held by Wittgenstein himself. Quite the reverse.

Let us return to consideration of the regress of justification.

6. REPLIES TO THE REGRESS ARGUMENT

An opponent of phenomenalism, in my broad sense, must deny that there are epistemologically basic beliefs. Let us call this alternative position 'the no foundations view'. Anyone who thinks that the regress argument forces us to recognize the existence of basic beliefs will think that this view involves a vicious infinite regress. But what is the cash-value of the claim that the no-foundations view is committed to the existence of a (potential) infinite regress of justification? Perhaps only this: that, according to the non-foundationalist, there are no privileged classes of beliefs such that 'ultimately' justification terminates with beliefs belonging to these classes. Most versions of phenomenalism recognize two such classes: certain kinds of perceptual beliefs, and beliefs which express analytic truths.

It is sometimes thought that one has only to point to the regress of justification in order to demonstrate the untenability of any non-foundationalist position. It is just obvious to writers like Price and Lewis that we must eventually come upon data which are 'data simpliciter'. But the argument cannot be allowed to move quite so quickly.

Clearly, any actual process of justification must terminate after finitely many steps. But what follows from this? Not very much. It shows at most, we can say, that at any given time we must have some stock of beliefs which are not thought to be open to challenge, though any one of them may subsequently come under fire. But the fact that justification must come to an end somewhere does not allow us to infer that the class of justification-terminating beliefs can be characterized in any non-trivial way. It would be clearly fallacious to argue that, since justification must come to an end somewhere, there must be some special kind of belief with which justification always terminates.

In this connexion, recall Chisholm's formulation of the doctrine of the given.[12] The essence of the doctrine, as Chisholm sees it, is that 'the knowledge which a person has at any time is a structure or edifice, many parts and stages of which help to support each other, but which as a whole is supported by its own foundation'. Now this statement of the doctrine *could* be interpreted along the anti-foundationalist lines just discussed. That is, it could be taken to assert no more than that, *at any time,* we must have some stock of well-entrenched beliefs which set the bounds within which current enquiry proceeds and which provide the touchstone for empirical justification. There is nothing in this to suggest that such beliefs must be intrinsically credible, that the foundation must be permanent, or that these beliefs must be of some special kind: say either first-person perceptual statements, or first-person memory statements. The point is that, unless one is careful to bear in mind just how much theoretical content is packed into Chisholm's notion of a 'foundation' for knowledge, his formulation of the doctrine of the given is likely to make that doctrine look much more obviously true and much more trivial than it really is. In fact, the doctrine is neither trivial nor, as I hope to show, is it true.

So far, we are allowing that basic beliefs may be defeasible. But this admission does not blunt the critical point developed above. For even a defender of phenomenalism who holds that basic beliefs are defeasible will claim that a basic belief has a logical presumption in favour of its being true. The idea of a logical presumption was explicated in terms of its being necessarily true that beliefs of a certain kind are for the most part true. But nothing has yet been done to show that there is a nontrivially characterizable kind to which our justification-terminating beliefs belong. Supposing these to be a fairly heterogeneous collection, it is implausible to claim that most of these, *as a matter of necessity,* are true. All might eventually be abandoned. Justification must terminate with beliefs for which there is a presumption in favour of their being true, but this does not have to be a logical presumption.

An important counter-move open to a defender of phenomenalism is to advance the claim that knowledge could not get off the ground unless there were epistemologically basic beliefs that were at least prima-facie justified, and this is why the regress of justification is intolerable. This kind of thing is said:

> Ordinarily, if we are appeared to redly we have no hesitation in judging that there is something red before us. We do not first try to establish that we are not hallucinating, that we are not wearing coloured glasses, that we are not hypnotized, that there are no coloured lights shining on the object, and so forth. These possibilities become relevant only if we have some concrete reason for thinking that one of them is actually the case. . . . If in making a perceptual judgment we had first to establish that none of the things that can go wrong with perception is going wrong, we could never get off the ground, because establishing, for example, that we are not hallucinating also involves perceptual judgments.[13]

---

[13] Taken from Pollock's 'Perceptual Knowledge'. Pollock, along with Chisholm and Bennett, is a prominent contemporary defender of an epistemological position which I should regard as a version of phenomenalism. He calls his approach 'descriptivism'; Chisholm calls his 'critical cognitivism'; Bennett calls his 'phenomenalism'. See also Pollock's 'Criteria and Our Knowledge of the Material World', *Philosophical Review*, 76 (1967), pp. 28–62.

These considerations are also adduced to show that not all the inferences we make can be empirically grounded. Some must be grounded in the meanings of the terms we use.

In reply, however, it could be said that none of this shows that *logical* presumptions or *logical* reasons have to get in on the act. Couldn't our lack of hesitation in making perceptual judgments when suitably appeared to be traced to certain beliefs about the world: e.g. the belief that hallucinations are relatively uncommon, as are gross defects in our perceptual apparatus, and so on.

I suggested earlier that the prima-facie credibility of perceptual judgments might be accounted for in terms of their being sincerely made being *empirically* sufficient for their being justified. A person's judgment that there is something red in front of him can be said to express observational knowledge because it is an instance of a tendency to make such judgments when and only when in the sensory state normally brought about by the presence of red objects. That such theories are possible is important because it shows that it is possible for certain judgments to be made credibly and 'without criteria', as one version of the regress argument has it, without their being intrinsically credible in any strong sense. The point is that particular tokens of a given type of judgment can be credible without there being criteria for them: their non-inferential credibility is simply a reflection of the fact that we are able to make true reports of that type 'without thinking about it'. This account of judgments made without criteria does not invoke the notion of intrinsic credibility: it appeals instead to empirical facts about the perceptual and linguistic capacities of human beings, especially their capacities for acquiring dispositions to respond directly to certain classes of stimuli.

However, to a defender of phenomenalism, this line of reply will only invite a reapplication of the original argument. For the relevant empirical facts are general facts, and how could knowledge of these be acquired? How could we ever be justified in holding such beliefs if we could not first be justified in holding certain particular perceptual beliefs? If this were not possible, knowledge could not get off the ground.

The dialectical pattern leading to the postulation of analytic evidential connexions is strikingly similar. To recall an earlier example, having a certain shape, colour and internal makeup may be supposed to constitute the criteria for being a tomato. Criteria are a kind of evidence and give us grounds for an inference to a belief in the existence of that for which they are criteria. But could this evidential relation hold in virtue of some general empirical feature of the world? That is, does observing that some object satisfies the criteria for being a tomato entitle us to judge that there is a tomato in the offing in the way that seeing smoke entitles us to expect fire? Surely not. If the evidential link between tomatoes and their criteria depended on some inductive correlation, we should face the threat of an infinite regress. To connect inductively the having of a certain shape, colour, and internal makeup with being a tomato, we need some independent way of knowing, in particular instances, that we have come across something which both satisfies the putative criteria *and is a tomato*: We need some evidence for something's being a tomato which is independent of the 'criteria' we want to validate. But in virtue of what does this 'evidence' count as evidence? Further empirical facts? We cannot have recourse to this reply indefinitely. Not everything we take to be evidence for something's being a tomato can reflect some inductively based correlation. If the enterprise of determining evidential relationships empirically is to be possible, there must be some evidential connexions that hold a priori and in virtue, not of fact, but of meaning. So the argument goes.

The non-foundationalist way of dealing with this argument parallels the response to the argument aiming to show that there must be epistemologically basic beliefs. All the argument shows, it may be said, is that not all of our beliefs about what counts as evidence for what can be put up for validation at once. Suppose that we establish inductively that Fs are reliable indicators of Gs. To do this, we must have some prior beliefs about what counts as good evidence for the presence of Fs and what counts in favour of the presence of Gs. But there is no need to take refuge in analytic connexions. Admittedly, we have to have some beliefs about what counts as evidence for Fs or Gs in order for the process of establishing a correlation to get off the ground—we have to have criteria for Fs and Gs. But these evidential relationships do not have to hold necessarily, and they can be given up. For example, once the correlation is established, we may come to take the presence of an F as the criterion for the presence of a G, and maybe give up the original criterion altogether. To insist that the evidential relationships hold analytically leads to the implausible view that every change of criterion involves a change of meaning. For example, we should have to hold, as did Norman Malcolm, that psychologists who study dreaming and who take rapid eye movements during sleep, amongst other things, to be criterial for the subject's having a dream, don't mean by 'dreaming' what ordinary people mean.[14]

Another way of putting this point is to say that the argument for the existence of analytic evidential connexions simply shows that we must not confuse a relationship's holding, in a sense, a priori with its holding necessarily, or in virtue of meaning. The threat of the regress shows that not all of our beliefs about what counts as evidence for what can have been established empirically: so we might say that some such beliefs are a priori relative to a given body of theory or area of enquiry. But a belief can be a priori in this sense and still be open to revision on empirical grounds. Thus showing that a belief is (relatively) a priori does not amount to

[14] Norman Malcolm, *Dreaming* (London: Routledge, 1959).

showing that it takes for its object an analytic truth. To make progress in this direction, it would have to be shown that some such beliefs are tenable absolutely a priori. The pro-phenomenalist argument breaks down just because it tries to move from something's being relatively a priori to its being absolutely a priori and true in virtue of meaning.

Underlying the argument is an assumption that every evidential connexion must hold either inductively or else analytically. The line of defence sketched out above consists essentially in resisting having this dichotomy foisted on us. The idea is that a distinction between evidential relations correlationally established and relations not so established is quite adequate to dispose of the threat of the regress.[15] But is there nothing to be said for the 'inductive or analytic' dichotomy? Consider the following reply: you admit that in order for the process of establishing correlations inductively to get off the ground we must have prior beliefs about evidential relationships. But these beliefs could not have been arrived at inductively: at least we must eventually come upon some that were not so established. How is such knowledge possible, if not in virtue of knowing what we mean? We have reached a position similar to that reached in the argument over whether we must recognize the existence of epistemologically basic beliefs.

7. Two Forms of the Regress Argument

The non-foundationalist view of knowledge which began to emerge in the preceding sections seems to imply that the process of acquiring new knowledge requires that a good number of things be already known. A similar implication can be seen to lurk in any view of meaning which denies that

---

[15] These issues are interestingly discussed by Richard Rorty in 'Criteria and Necessity', NOUS, (1973) pp. 313-329.

it is possible to have only epistemologically basic beliefs. Don't we therefore have an argument in favour of phenomenalism—i.e. that, if the no foundations view were correct, the process of acquiring knowledge could never get off the ground? Let us call this 'the genetic argument'.

It is worth emphasizing that the genetic argument presupposes a picture of the acquisition of knowledge which takes seriously the idea that there could be a first belief or at least a state of having only basic beliefs. So a defence of phenomenalism via recourse to the genetic argument commits one to regarding epistemologically basic beliefs as beliefs which could justifiably be held even in the absence of further beliefs, or at least further non-basic beliefs. This in turn requires a rejection of the attractive idea that the meaning of a belief is a function of its role in thought. That idea leads to a holistic view of meaning and of belief which suggests that what a person means and what he believes to be true do not constitute neatly separable components of knowledge: the phenomenalist picture requires just the opposite.

The phenomenalist picture is also supported by a particular theory of memory: that one can be said to remember only what one has previously known.[16] If this were true, there would indeed have to be a first episode of knowing.

However, it should be clear that the genetic argument cannot force us to adopt a phenomenalist position, for the picture of the acquisition of knowledge it presupposes is not the only one available. In fact, the arguments which are supposed to compel the recognition of epistemologically basic beliefs and analytic evidential connexions can be turned on their heads. In defence of the no-foundations view, we

---

[16] Thought at one time to be obviously true. For an influential statement of this view see Norman Malcolm, 'Three Lectures on Memory', in *Knowledge and Certainty*.

can say that the fact we need to have a good number of beliefs in order for the process of acquiring new knowledge empirically to get off the ground shows that our belief system must, to an extent, emerge whole.[17] The phenomenalist view assumes that the process of acquiring knowledge could get off the ground only if there were initial beliefs from which to proceed by analytically validated steps. But it can be said in reply that the pro-phenomenalist arguments show only that the complex system of linguistic and other dispositions which eventually come to constitute knowledge cannot be seen as the end product of first acquiring little bits of knowledge and gradually integrating them, by various inferential moves, into a more complex whole. In other words, the no-foundations view can be defended by claiming that a person becomes a full-fledged knower only when his linguistic and other practices have reached a degree of complexity sufficient for it to be apparent that he accepts sentences of many different kinds, that he has various general as well as particular beliefs. But stages on the road to this state are not themselves states of knowledge of some more primitive kind, differing from the final state only in the number of beliefs involved and the types of belief represented, even though such pre-cognitive experience may be the causal antecedent of what later comes to be knowledge. This alternative picture suggests that the theory of memory implicit in the phenomenalist picture is too restrictive. It is quite possible for me to have non-inferential memory knowledge of events which I did not know at the time to be taking place because, lacking the necessary conceptual abilities, I was not in a position to *know* anything of the sort.

If the gradualist theory of the acquisition of knowledge

---

[17] Cf. Wittgenstein: 'When we begin to *believe* anything, what we believe is not a single proposition, it is a whole system of propositions'. *On Certainty* (New York: J. and J. Harper, 1969), No. 141.

presupposed by the genetic argument were the only possible view of the matter, then it would indeed be hard to see how we could get off the ground unless some kind of phenomenalist theory were correct. But it is not the only view of the matter. Worse still, it is tied up with the traditional doctrine of the given.

How is it possible to start off by having only basic observational knowledge? The doctrine of the given provides the answer. The first step towards acquiring a language and linguistically formulated knowledge is one of mastering a stock of basic observational predicates. The use of such predicates, with their full determinate meanings, can be acquired ab initio just because the meanings of these predicates are fixed ostensively. On this view, learning the meanings of basic observational predicates is a matter of inductive inference, of correlating certain sounds (utterances of words) with various sensible qualities of which we are prelinguistically aware. This account of how meanings are learned is just a genetic analogue of Ayer's second kind of linguistic rule, the kind which correlates 'symbols' with 'observable facts'. Here we have an appeal to the doctrine of the given in its strongest form.

We can distinguish at least two kinds of awareness: awareness as discriminative reaction, and whatever 'higher' kind is required for the existence of knowledge. This latter kind of awareness presupposes the exercise of concepts, and to exercise concepts one must possess a measure of linguistic competence. No doubt we could never get to this stage without an initial capacity for awareness of the first kind; that is to say, without an initial capacity to respond differentially to different stimuli. The kind of awareness we are supposed to have in our encounter with the sensibly given seems to be some kind of intermediate case: more than a capacity for discriminative response, and yet less than fully fledged propositional knowledge. We saw in chapter two how difficult it is to make anything of this idea. However, unless this idea were lurking in the background, I do not think that the genetic argument could ever look to have much plausibility.

The line that I have taken so far against the genetic argument is essentially that followed by Sellars. However, I do not think that his discussion is entirely adequate. According to Sellars' account of observational knowledge, utterances of sentences like 'This is green' can be said to express observational knowledge only if the speaker knows that such utterances are reliable indicators of the presence of green objects in conditions standard for visual perception. He adds this condition because he feels that the ability to respond reliably is insufficient for knowledge: for a report to express knowledge, it is not sufficient that it be reliable, its reliability must also be recognized by the speaker. Sellars is concerned to rebut the objection that his theory involves a regress:

> And it might be thought that there is an obvious regress in the view we are examining. Does it not tell us that observational knowledge at time t presupposes knowledge of the form 'X is a reliable symptom of Y', which presupposes prior observational knowledge, which presupposes *other* knowledge of the form 'X is a reliable symptom of Y', which presupposes still other, and *prior,* observational knowledge, and so on?[18]

The objection Sellars considers is clearly a version of what I have called 'the genetic argument'. His reply is that it

> . . . rests on too simple, indeed a radically mistaken conception of what one is saying of Jones when one says that he *knows* that-p. . . . The essential point is that in characterizing an episode or a state as that of *knowing,* we are not giving an empirical description of that episode or

[18] Sellars, op. cit., pp. 168-169.

state; we are placing it in the logical space of reasons, of justifying and being able to justify what one says.

Thus, all that the view I am defending requires is that no tokening by S *now* of 'This is green' is to count as 'expressing observational knowledge' unless it is also correct to say of S that he *now* knows the appropriate fact of the form 'X is a reliable symptom of Y', namely that . . . utterances of 'This is green' are reliable indicators of the presence of green objects in standard conditions of perception. And while the correctness of this statement about Jones requires that Jones could *now* cite prior particular facts as evidence for the idea that these utterances *are* reliable indicators, it requires only that it is correct to say that Jones *now* knows, thus remembers, that these particular facts *did* obtain. It does not require that it be correct to say that at the time these facts did obtain he *then knew* them to obtain. And the regress disappears.[19]

However, there is another way to react to the genetic argument. This is to deny that a person need always be able to justify an assertion in order for it to count as an expression of knowledge. Thus we might count a child's early observation reports as expressing knowledge because they are *in fact* reliable (and are justifiable by a fully-fledged language-user, thus making the child a *potential* justifier) even though the child could not be expected to marshal facts about his perceptual and linguistic capabilities in support of his observational claims. Once again, this involves no concession to the foundational view of knowledge. If we do not require that the justification for these early expressions of belief be known, the fact that we allow there to be first episodes of non-inferential knowing will not help to show that there are epistemologically basic beliefs in any interesting sense. For if we insist only that these early reports

---

[19] Ibid., p. 169.

be in fact reliable, and do not insist that the speaker be able to justify reliance on them, then we can still give an empirical account of the credibility and non-inferential character of observation reports along the lines suggested by Sellars. This account is anti-foundationalist in that it traces the credibility of observation reports to facts knowledge of which would not be basic by anyone's standards.

I think, then, that we can go either way. If we agree that knowing always requires being able to justify, we will follow Sellars and deny that our present knowledge of certain general facts like 'X is a reliable symptom of Y' depends on our having had *prior knowledge* of the relevant particular facts. We will say that our ability to give reasons *now* is built on a long history of language-learning, certain episodes in which—e.g. utterances of 'This is green'—were no doubt 'superficially like those which are later properly said to express observational knowledge'. But the likeness is superficial. In the absence of the ability to justify, it would be incorrect to describe such episodes as expressions of observational knowledge. On the other hand, if we do not insist quite so rigorously on the ability to justify, we can allow that these earlier episodes, the ones which Sellars thinks are only 'superficially like' expressions of observational knowledge properly so-called, to count as genuine expressions of knowledge, without thereby committing ourselves to a foundationalist account of their credibility. Sellars' approach to the genetic argument is the one to take if we insist on a strict application of the principle that knowing requires more than the ability to respond reliably—specifically that it requires the ability to justify. However, against the plausibility of this aspect of Sellars' position must be weighed what can seem a counter intuitive consequence: that the infant who says 'Mama'—can say little else—does not mean 'mother'. In fact, Sellars' view that such infantile utterances are only 'superficially like' genuine expressions of observational knowledge would seem to imply that the infant does not mean anything, but is merely 'parroting'. If this consequence strikes us as overly para- doxical, we can take the more relaxed approach to the genetic argument sketched above. I do not choose between these two approaches because I have no clear intuitions about how much justifying a person has to be able to do before he counts as knowing. For my purpose, the important point is that, no matter which position we take on this issue, the genetic argument can be defeated.

One thing that emerges from the foregoing discussion is that Sellars must be wrong to trace the genetic argument to 'a radically mistaken conception of what one is saying of Jones when one says that he knows that-p.' On the contrary, if it is to support foundationalism, the argument must incorporate a view of knowledge very like Sellars' own. That is, the argument's implication that there must be intrinsically credible basic beliefs depends on its assuming (1) that we only have knowledge if we are actually in possession of the justification for our beliefs, which is pretty much the position that Sellars himself takes, and (2) that we can only have knowledge of general facts—facts like 'X is a reliable symptom of Y'—if we have had *prior observational knowledge* of the relevant particular facts. Both premises are essential to the argument, as is shown by the fact that denying either one is sufficient to defeat it; and taken together they do imply that the beliefs we start from must constitute knowledge in virtue of being intrinsically credible. In Chisholm's phrase, they must describe states that are 'self-presenting'. Sellars' strategy for dealing with the genetic argument is to deny (2) and to claim that, since knowing requires being able to justify, our *knowledge* of the particular general facts in question emerges all at once, everything else being a non-cognitive causal antecedent. I have argued that it may also be possible to turn the genetic argument by denying (1).

I conclude that, so far, we have not seen any reason to

suppose that some version of phenomenalism has to be correct. On the contrary, since arguments for this position lead us back towards the doctrine of the given, we have reason to think that the no-foundations view of knowledge is to be preferred.

To many defenders of phenomenalism, the defeat of the genetic argument will seem no great loss. It is widely held that 'genetic' considerations have no place in epistemology. No doubt there have been a great many philosophers who have concerned themselves with the 'origins' of knowledge, Locke and Hume being notable examples, but it is often said that, insofar as their purposes were genuinely philosophical, they mistook the nature of their enterprise. Epistemology proper is concerned not with the origins of knowledge, but with the nature or structure of the justification for our most important beliefs, our belief in the existence of the physical world for example. This view of epistemology was foreshadowed in section three where I suggested that a phenomenalist objects to there being even a potential regress of justification.

The charge of irrelevant geneticism, or psychologism, has probably been levelled more against Hume than against any other single philosopher. To my mind, this meta-philosophical prejudice has made cogent discussion of some of Hume's most interesting ideas all but impossible. Bennett sums up the modern consensus when he says that the 'crucial trouble' with Hume's theory of ideas is that it is 'genetic rather than analytic'.[20] However, I think that we should view this dichotomy with some suspicion. At first glance, it is not easy to see why 'analytic' should be contrasted with 'genetic' at all. It looks as though two distinctions (or alleged distinctions) have been run together: the distinction between analytic and synthetic (or empirical) truths, and the distinction between questions concerning

[20] Bennett, op. cit., p. 230.

justification (say, of our beliefs about the physical world) and questions concerning the origins of such beliefs. The idea that distinctively epistemological theories are analytic rather than genetic assumes (i) that questions of justification rather than questions of origins are the proper concern of epistemology, and (ii) that the former, when philosophical, are to be answered 'analytically' and the latter empirically. Both assumptions are false. Theories which account for the credibility attaching to beliefs of a certain type by arguing that such beliefs are the outcome of a reliable process or method—Hume's theory of causal inference and Sellars' account of observational knowledge could be taken as examples—are theories of justification which appeal to facts about the origins of those beliefs. They are thus both genetic and empirical. But for all that, they answer questions about justification.

The metaphilosophical thesis that such empirical theories have no place in epistemology is plausible only given a prior commitment to a foundational view of knowledge. If we take 'justifying' our beliefs about the physical world to be a matter of showing how such beliefs are related to a privileged fund of epistemologically prior basic knowledge, then it will seem that any straightforward appeal to matters of empirical fact in order to answer questions about 'justification' will be question-begging, since such an appeal will simply bring forward further examples of the kind of belief whose 'justification' is in question. The idea that it makes sense to ask for the justification of *all* such beliefs all at once, and the idea that 'justifying' them consists in placing them on their proper foundation are two sides of the same coin. Nothing testifies more strongly to the vacuity of the question than the answers forced upon us by the view of justification upon which the question depends. Thus we are told that the basic data are simply *given* (and are thus absolutely non-inferential), or that the data confer warrant on higher-level beliefs through links which hold in virtue of meaning (and are thus absolutely a priori). I think that such explanations are quite without content. But once we agree that epistemological questions lie, in Price's phrase, 'outside the sphere of science altogether', it is hard to see what else we might say.

The genetic argument failed to yield a conclusive result in favour of phenomenalism. But there is another, non-genetic, aspect to the disquiet that a defender of phenomenalism may feel at the prospect of there being a regress of justification. To a defender of a no-foundations view, he might want to say something like this: 'In order to justify beliefs of a given type, you always appeal to some of your other beliefs—but what justifies the whole thing, according to your theory? However, in view of the argument just given, I think that we should be suspicious of attempts to interpret the regress argument non-genetically. What else could justification consist in if not bringing accepted beliefs forward in support of the propositions to be justified? Insofar as we can make sense of the idea of justifying the whole thing, it seems that the notion of 'justification' in play is exactly that required by the foundational view which lies at the heart of phenomenalism: and this is just what we want an argument for. If 'How do you justify the whole thing?' means 'How do you place it on its proper foundation?', we can ask, in reply, 'Why should we want to?' If this is right, the genetic argument, far from being of minor importance, could be the only argument there is for adopting a phenomenalistic view of knowledge.

Still, let us see what we can make of non-genetic arguments for the foundational view of knowledge. The point of the question 'What justifies the whole system?' has often been to suggest that acceptance of a no-foundations view commits one to a coherence theory of justification;[21]

---

[21] Instead of 'coherence theory of justification' I could have said 'coherence theory of truth' since much of the traditional debate over the correspondence versus coherence theory of truth has really been about

and the coherence theory, it is said, 'cuts justification off from the world'.[22]

A first reaction to this charge is to say that it is entirely misconceived. I have suggested that a natural strategy for a

justification. This is because philosophical theories of truth have been seen not only as giving competing accounts of the 'nature' of truth but also as offering alternative criteria or tests of truth. In fact, the debate between correspondence and coherence theorists was mainly centred around the question of whether knowledge has to be seen as founded on given facts.

It should be obvious that adopting correspondence as the test of truth leads straight away to a foundational view of knowledge, indeed to the doctrine of the given in its strongest form. To borrow an example from Blanshard, we do not know to be true the statement 'Burr killed Hamilton in a duel' in virtue of having checked that this statement corresponds with a fact: the fact to which it corresponds is no longer available for inspection. If we are to adopt correspondence as a test of truth, we must define a privileged class of statements capable of verification by direct comparison with the facts and these will determine the ultimate evidence on which all our more 'theoretical' knowledge must rest. Of course, in view of this, it is reasonable to ask why anyone should ever want to put forward correspondence as the test of truth. One reason is that it is natural to think that if the test of truth were to have no essential connection with the nature of truth, then it would appear wildly paradoxical that we ever have any knowledge at all. Put another way, if coherence were the test of truth and correspondence its nature, what would make coherence a test of *truth*? And buried beneath this worry is the picture discussed in the text of our beliefs forming a network floating above the world and needing some point of contact, some point at which thought can touch reality. This point of contact is provided by the range of given facts and these in turn define the level at which correspondence can function as a test.

Nowadays, it is becoming popular to distinguish sharply between the theory of truth and the theory of evidence. Whether this is legitimate is a difficult question and one I shall not take up here. However, this much seems clear: that if the theory of truth is sharply distinguished from the theory of evidence, theories of truth have nothing to tell us about epistemological problems. This is true of Tarski's theory, the paradigm of modern theories of truth, and also, I think, of work in the so-called theory of reference, though to offer a detailed defence of this opinion would take me too far afield. For an opposing view see Hartry Field, 'Tarksi's Theory of Truth', *Journal of Philosophy*, July 1972.

[22] For a recent presentation of this argument, see Pollock's 'Perceptual Knowledge'. This idea figured prominently in C. I. Lewis's epistemological thought.

defender of a no-foundations view is to offer an empirical account of the credibility of perceptual reports. Far from cutting justification off from the world, an account along these lines will show how our encounter with the physical world through perception leads to justified belief.

The problem with this, from the standpoint of a defender of phenomenalism, is that it looks as if the relevant relations of justification go around in a circle: a general theory underpins the credibility of particular perceptual reports. But doesn't the credibility of such a theory rest ultimately on particular observations?

At this point, the question 'What justifies the whole thing?' can seem particularly pressing. One can become haunted by the picture of one's beliefs system incorporating all sorts of internal relations of justification while, as a whole, floating above the world with no point of contact. But this worry is incoherent, because the concept of 'the world' which is operative here is completely vacuous.[23] As soon as we start thinking of that with which belief has to make contact as congeries of elementary particles, patterns of retinal irradiation, or relational arrays of sensuous colour-patches, we are operating within some particular theory of the way the world is, and the question of how belief relates to the world no longer seems puzzling. The question can exert its paralysing effect only as long as (and indeed because) the notion of 'the world' is allowed to remain as the notion of something completely unspecifiable.

The unspecifiability of the world is of a piece with the ineffability of the given. Writers like Lewis clearly think that our confrontation with the sensibly given constitutes the point of contact between thought and the world. Only thus is knowledge saved from being 'contentless and arbitrary'. A recent advocate of such a view is Jonathan Bennett. He

---

[23] Here I am indebted to Richard Rorty. See 'The World Well Lost', *Journal of Philosophy*, 69, 19 (1972), pp. 649–65.

endorses 'a general empiricism about all meanings', the thesis that

> . . . to understand any statement, I must be able to connect the difference between its truth and falsity with some difference it could make to me—some difference in the data, the raw chunks of reality, with which I am confronted, i.e. in the sensory states which I have or, as Berkeley would say, in the ideas I perceive.[24]

Of course, confronting raw chunks of reality gets us no further than Ayer's rules which correlate symbols with ineffable observable facts, or Price's 'pure' inspection, or Bradley's component of knowledge known only as 'this'. That is to say, it gets us nowhere. For if this confronting of the world, of reality, is to serve as a check upon belief, to be in effect the ultimate standard by which true knowledge is separated from idle fancy, then this activity must involve judgment. So we have a dilemma: either our confrontation with the given is just one more variety of perceptual judgment, in which case we no longer have a point of pure contact between the mind and the world, or else the content of the given is ineffable, in which case it cannot provide a rational check on anything, cannot favour one hypothesis over another.

Our awareness of the sensibly given is a non-propositional grasping of an unspecifiable world. No wonder it is ineffable. Of course, this position cannot be maintained: nothing can be done if the nature of the reality we confront is left so utterly vague. The difficulty is illustrated graphically by the passage quoted from Bennett: after insisting on the need to confront 'raw' chunks of reality, he goes on to tell us that this activity consists in the 'having' of sensory states or, in Berkeley's terms, the perception of ideas.

The picture of our belief-system floating above 'the world'

[24] Bennett, op. cit. p. 136.

and the attempt to establish a point of contact by an appeal to the given lead us into a blind alley. The charge that, unless some version of phenomenalism were true, justification would be cut off from 'the world' fails because either the notion of 'the world' in play here is the notion of something completely unspecifiable, an unknowable thing-in-itself, in which case the charge is unintelligible, or else we are dealing with the notion of 'the world' as it is according to some particular theory, in which case the charge is not true.

However, perhaps we can just forget about 'the world', the given, and so on. Surely the substance of the charge that justification would be cut off from the world is that, if the coherence theory were true, one could be justified in believing anything at all, provided that the belief in question could be incorporated into a, no doubt outlandish, but still coherent set of beliefs. Thus Pollock argues that, if the coherence theory were correct, then a person could be justified in believing that all of his senses mislead him all of the time: but this is impossible, so the coherence theory cannot be correct.[25] It may be true, a defender of phenomenalism might say, that certain philosophers have got this point entangled with a desire to 'get outside language' or to confront 'raw chunks of reality', but this is not an essential feature of the pro-phenomenalist argument.

It is sometimes thought that this argument establishes the need for a class of incorrigible beliefs. Thus Schlick held that the possibility of there being an indefinite number of equally good total belief-systems was absurd and concluded that

> . . . the only way to avoid this absurdity is not to allow that any statements whatever can be abandoned or altered, but rather to specify those that are to be maintained, to which the remainder are to be accommodated.[26]

[25] Pollock, 'Perceptual Knowledge', p. 291.
[26] Moritz Schlick, 'The Foundation of Knowledge'. Originally

Those that are to be maintained turn out to be observation statements, which Schlick calls 'confirmations', and which are understood by comparing them with 'the facts'. But why should this be so? I think that Schlick commits a version of the fallacy noted earlier: that of concluding from the fact that justification must terminate somewhere that there must be some particular kind of belief with which it terminates. In reply to the observation that justification must come to an end somewhere, I noted that the most that we can conclude from this is that at any given time we must have some stock of beliefs not thought to be open to challenge, though any one of them may subsequently come under fire. Any one can be questioned, though not all can be questioned at once. In reply to Schlick, a similar argument is in order: our stock of well-entrenched beliefs—a body of scientific theory, common platitudes, unquestioned perceptual reports, and so on—constitute those being maintained, to which the less certain remainder have to be accommodated. Of course, there is no guarantee that there will be a unique best way of accommodating them, and there will always be room for disagreement. But this is hardly an absurdity. And if it were, recourse to an incorrigible body of confirmations would not save us from it. For why should we suppose that there is a unique best way of accommodating 'the remainder' to them? There is no reason. Even Schlick's own theory cannot hope to meet the stringent conditions he lays down.

A further point to notice about certain popular arguments is that it is generally assumed that coherence amounts to nothing more than logical consistency.[27] Schlick certainly

published in German in *Erkenntnis* (1934). A translation is to be found in Ayer (ed.), *Logical Positivism* (New York: Free Press, 1959). Quotation from p. 216. The clash between foundationalism and the coherence theory looms large in the debate between various positivists over whether just any sentence could be a protocol, and over the question of whether truth was a matter of 'correspondence'. In addition to Schlick's article, see papers (in the Ayer volume) by Carnap, Neurath, and Ayer.

[27] C. I. Lewis is an exception. He thought that our various beliefs must

assumes as much. This is quite unfair to coherence theorists. Bradley, for example, was quite explicit in his view that more than mere consistency was required. This something more he called 'comprehensiveness'.[28] By 'comprehensiveness' he meant something like 'explanatory coherence': our beliefs must not just be consistent, they must also hang together theoretically. Blanshard, too, had something similar in mind when he wrote of the need for 'unity and conclusiveness'[29] in an acceptable body of beliefs. If we replace consistency by explanatory coherence, there is no longer any plausibility to the claim that the coherence theory makes it possible to believe with justification any consistent fairy story. When listening to or reading a fairy story, the question 'How could that happen?' is quite inappropriate, which is just to say that fairy stories are not, and are not meant to be, coherent in the required sense. Neither is it obvious that any belief whatsoever can be incorporated into some coherent system of beliefs. On the contrary, it is open to a defender of the coherence theory to argue that the fact that certain ideas strike us as absurd—e.g. that there could be a system of beliefs which made plausible the supposition that all of our senses mislead us all of the time—is evidence that such systems could not really be coherent. How else could one hope to say in more detail what coherence adds up to? Our actual inferential practices provide the only evidence there is to go on.[30]

also probabilify one another. But he did not think that this made any difference to the question in hand, no doubt in part because he thought that if nothing is certain, nothing else is even truly probable.

[28] F. H. Bradley, *Essays on Truth and Reality* (Oxford: Clarendon Press, 1914).

[29] Brand Blanshard, *The Nature of Thought* (London: Allen and Unwin, 1939). For his views on truth see esp. chs. 25 and 26. I regret not having read Blanshard before this book was complete in draft.

[30] This strategy for epistemological argument is endorsed by Blanshard and by Harman in *Thought*. An influential proponent of such a view has been Nelson Goodman: see *Fact, Fiction and Forecast* (New York: Bobbs-Merrill, 1965).

Be that as it may, even consistency alone imposes stronger constraints on belief than is commonly realized. At least, it does so once we remove an unrealistic restriction implicit in the kind of argument advanced by Schlick. When Schlick claims that, if the coherence theory were true, we could believe any consistent fairy story with as much justification as we have for believing our most strongly supported scientific theories, he is tacitly confining his attention to systems of belief containing only beliefs of the first order —that is, beliefs about objects in the world, as opposed to 'second-order', we might say 'epistemic', beliefs about those beliefs. But since any rational system of beliefs must allow for its own change and development, and for the justification of the beliefs it contains, it is clear that such a system cannot contain only first-order beliefs but must also contain second-order beliefs about techniques for acquiring beliefs. Examples of such beliefs are to be found in those beliefs about the reliability of perception which underpin our claims to non-inferential perceptual knowledge.

The need for second-order beliefs could be represented as a dimension of 'coherence', in fact one of the most important dimensions, in that second-order beliefs figure centrally in the giving of justifications. A miscellany of first-order beliefs, or a fairy story, will not allow for much in the way of justification-relations between its various components and so will not 'hang together'. And indeed, it is only because of our holding epistemic beliefs that, say, the acceptance or rejection of a particular perceptual belief can have far-reaching systematic import. However, the point I want to emphasize here is that once we admit that, if we want to talk about justification or change of belief, we must deal with beliefs of the second as well as the first order, consistency alone exercises a much more powerful re-straining influence. The easy counter-examples sought by Schlick are no longer forthcoming. Presumably he does not intend that if we accept a consistent fairy story we also accept the principle that it is all right to accept any consistent fairy story we happen to hear or make up. We could not even *consistently* do this. But then what beliefs about techniques for acquiring beliefs are we supposed to accept? We could not, having accepted a story in which pots talk and frogs turn into princes, hold on to our usual beliefs about observational knowledge, for these would soon convince us that such things simply don't happen. Serious counter-examples to the coherence theory are more difficult to come by than some of that theory's opponents have supposed.[31]

Another feature of the pro-phenomenalist argument is that it presupposes a view of meaning which allows what a person means and what he believes to enjoy a high degree of mutual independence. Take Pollock's case of the man who believes that all of his senses mislead him all of the time. When he says 'It looks to me as if there is a duck over there', he is not giving voice to a belief which for him provides a prima-facie reason to think that there really is a duck over there. When he believes that it looks to him as if there is something red before him he does not thereby acquire a reason to believe that he is actually seeing something red, and so on. Nevertheless, we are invited to suppose that his beliefs, even though they lack their usual inferential functions, and even though we should have great difficulty

[31] It won't do to offer as a counter-example to the coherence theory a situation in which we have competing theories which, as the given stage of enquiry, we cannot choose between. This is a possibility which any reasonable epistemology must allow for and, as I argued in the text, even Schlick's does so. The natural candidates are various Cartesian examples—brains in vats, nasty deities and so on. But such examples are far more problematic for a foundational view of knowledge than for a coherence theory because the former requires us to rule them out on a much more restricted evidential basis. In fact, as I showed in chapter one, Cartesian examples only raise the threat of radical scepticism in the context of a prior commitment to the foundational view. From the point of view of the coherence theory, such examples are invariably underdescribed. How does the deception work (in detail)? Why does God treat us this way? And so on.

construing them in the desired way, still have the same content as the beliefs which we should express in the same words. Unless it is possible for meaning to remain invariant under extensive and systematic change of belief, the kind of example in question will not show that the coherence makes it possible to believe anything you like.

If there is a limit to the amount of change of belief under which meaning can plausibly be held to remain invariant, then it is not even obviously true that, for a given set of beliefs we are inclined to accept, there are just any number of consistent, let alone coherent, sets of further beliefs into which these beliefs might be incorporated. For a sufficiently radical change in the body of beliefs in which they are incorporated will call in question the claim that their meaning has remained the same.

One result of this is that the coherence theory does not offer itself as a defence against cognitive anarchy in quite the same way as does phenomenalism. For the coherence theory does not recognize the same degree of potential instability as the arguments adduced to discredit the coherence theory and motivate phenomenalism suggest that there is. So the coherence theory has less to defend against than does phenomenalism.

This is not a knockdown refutation of the attack on the coherence theory, since it is simply not clear in advance how much change of belief we are prepared to tolerate before we decide that the rational course is to think up some new way of deciding what is meant. But, equally, the fact that it is not clear is sufficient to rule out a confident appeal to cases like that of the man who believes that all of his senses mislead him all of the time as a knockdown refutation of the coherence theory.

A confident appeal to cases where everything seems the same but is construed differently is possible if one is prepared to defend the empiricist account of the meanings of basic observational terms which has surfaced from time to time throughout this chapter. If one holds that the meanings of such terms are fixed ostensively, then it is indeed possible to hold that their meanings are determinate in the mind independently of any scheme for translation. If acceptable, such a view would make our reaction to the case of the man who believes that all of his senses mislead him all of the time seem quite misguided. For what we were worrying about was how we might construe his expressions of belief, whereas what matters is what *he* means.

In addition to its internal problems, this view of meaning produces more difficulties than it solves. A well known example is the inverted spectrum problem. How do I know that the colours I am aware of in certain circumstances do not differ in a systematic way from those of which other people are aware, such that I mean by 'red' what they mean by 'green' and so on? The possibility of raising such questions seriously is itself a count against the empiricist view of how predicates like 'red' get their meaning. But its acceptance is required only if certain arguments are to be deployed against the no-foundations view of knowledge. As in the case of the genetic argument, consideration of the ideas which underpin the phenomenalist position lead us back to the doctrine of the given.

There is, however, a far more damaging criticism which can be levelled at Pollock's argument: that it is not an argument for the foundational view at all. Pollock argues as follows:

> As long as a person's beliefs form . . . a coherent set, he could hold any beliefs at all regarding the colours, shapes, sizes, and so forth of things, regardless of how they look or feel to him. Given . . . a coherence theory of justification, we could well imagine a person whose beliefs were such as to justify him in rejecting all of the evidence of his senses. For example, he might justifiably believe that whatever looks tall is really short, whatever looks red

is really blue, whatever looks green is really yellow, whatever feels hot is really cold, and so forth. As long as his beliefs form a coherent set there would be nothing wrong with this. The person would be justified in believing that all of his senses mislead him in a systematic way. Notice that this is not simply a matter of his rejecting all of the evidence of his senses and adopting a sceptical stance. He has positive beliefs concerning precisely how his senses mislead him. But I submit that it is impossible for him to be justified in holding such a set of beliefs. A person may well be justified in believing that some particular sense misleads him in some particular way. For example, a colour-blind person can know that he is colour-blind. But he can know that only by relying upon other evidence of his senses. It is impossible for a person to be justified in believing that *all* of his senses systematically mislead him *all* of the time. And yet this sort of thing would be possible if the nebula theory [Pollock's term for the no-foundations view] were correct. Therefore, the nebula theory cannot be correct. An infinite regress of justification is impossible. All justification must eventually terminate with some epistemologically basic beliefs which do not require independent justification. And at least some of these must have something to do with the evidence of our senses.[32]

In spite of the resounding conclusion, this is simply not an argument for the existence of epistemologically basic beliefs. Suppose that we admit that there are such beliefs, and that they have to do with how things look, feel, and so on. The person in Pollock's example has any number of such beliefs—that things look tall, look red, feel hot, and so forth. He accepts the evidence of his senses in that he entertains beliefs about how things look just as we do, and it

---

[32] Pollock, 'Perceptual Knowledge', pp. 291-92.

is quite consistent with the example to suppose that these beliefs 'do not require independent justification'. The problem is that he infers a total account of his sensory evidence which justifies him in believing that a thing's looking red, say, gives no reason for supposing that it really is red. He does not reject the sensory evidence per se: he only rejects it as evidence for our standard view of the objective world. Allowing that beliefs about this sensory evidence are epistemologically basic, in the sense of not requiring independent justification, does not clear up the puzzle set by Pollock's example. For the difficulty springs not from a failure to recognize the epistemologically basic status of sensory evidence, but from the peculiar *inference* which is made on the basis of that evidence.

Pollock's argument, then, does not count in favour of the existence of epistemologically basic beliefs. The puzzle does not depend on denying that there are such beliefs. Their existence can be conceded and the example, and the puzzle it points to, left unchanged. More than this, however, I think that Pollock gets things exactly backwards. Far from depending on a denial of the claim that beliefs having to do with the evidence of the senses are epistemologically basic, the example presupposes that they are. The puzzle it sets is that of showing why it is impossible for a person to be justified in believing that all of his senses mislead him all of the time. Pollock's character accepts the evidence of his senses but infers a total account of this evidence which justifies him in believing that it is systematically misleading. But the example assumes that forming justified beliefs about the objective world is a matter of inferring these beliefs from a basis of purely sensory evidence. The problem is to show how this evidence can point one way rather than another, and this is not a problem we have to face unless we assume that justification terminates ultimately with such sensory evidence. In effect, Pollock presents a variation on the argument for radical scepticism which we examined in chapter one. The argument says: given that all of our knowledge of the objective world rests ultimately on a foundation of beliefs about how things look, feel and so on, show why it is correct to infer our standard view rather than one which strikes us as absurd. Thus the way Pollock describes his example embodies an implicit commitment to the foundational view from the outset. It is not an argument in favour of that view. In fact, since the foundational view can be used to generate such absurd conclusions, it is an argument against it. One way to avoid these conclusions, and the one which Pollock himself advocates, is to claim that there are evidential connexions which hold in virtue of meaning, and which connect beliefs about the objective world with the basic sensory evidence. But this is an argument in favour of a particular kind of foundational theory, given that some kind of foundational theory has to be correct. It is an argument to the effect that, once the foundational picture has been accepted, an appeal to truth in virtue of meaning is not to be avoided. This too is a count against accepting the foundational view. But the important point is that, however we try to construe Pollock's argument, it does not count in favour of the foundational view: it presupposes it.

To conclude this chapter, I want to raise the following question: If a 'theory of justification' is supposed to capture the essence of justification, does accepting a no-foundations view of knowledge commit one to a coherence theory of justification in any interesting sense? I argued that justification is a matter of accommodating beliefs that are being questioned to a body of accepted beliefs. Justification always terminates with other *beliefs* and not with our confronting 'raw chunks of reality', for that idea is incoherent. Neither have we seen any reason to suppose that justification must terminate always with beliefs drawn from some permanent body of purely observational knowledge. The beliefs which current inquiry is leaving alone can be of many different kinds. So does the coherence theory to which the no-foundations view is supposed to be committed amount to any more than a mere denial of the claim that knowledge has a foundation?

I see no reason why it should. Why should a rejection of the foundational view commit one to offering an alternative statement of the one thing justification ultimately consists in? To be sure, one can say that the essence of warranted inference is to increase explanatory coherence, but this is not a particularly interesting thing to say. In fact it has the kind of triviality which attaches to the claim that physicists study physical phenomena. When electromagnetic phenomena made their appearance on the scientific scene, physicists did not think that they now had to study two kinds of phenomena, the physical and the electromagnetic: rather they recognized the discovery of a new class of physical phenomena.[33]

Chisholm claims that many philosophers, especially those influenced by Dewey and Wittgenstein, have been critical of epistemological questions about justification because they have thought that to raise such questions is to imply that there is some real doubt about the validity of our beliefs about the physical world, other minds, and so on, or because they have thought that to raise such questions is to call for further verification. According to Chisholm, they have misconceived the character of the epistemological enterprise. The concern of epistemology is what Lewis called 'the critique of cogency'. Such a project presupposes that we are justified in holding most of the beliefs that we do hold: the idea is to discover the nature of this justification.[34]

---

[33] This example is borrowed from Harman, though he uses it in quite another connexion.

[34] Again, see his contribution to *The Princeton Studies*. Another compact statement of Chisholm's views can be found in his *Theory of Knowledge* (Englewood Cliffs, N.J.: Prentice-Hall, 1966).

But what is it to 'discover the nature of this justification'? It does not consist in investigating the reasons which people actually give for holding their various beliefs; rather the method employed is one of asking 'Socratic' questions about the justification for certain beliefs until eventually we come upon beliefs which are 'self-justifying'. Such beliefs constitute the proper stopping place for questions about justification.

Reichenbach once wrote that 'there is no Archimedean point of absolute certainty left to which to attach our knowledge of the world; all we have is an elastic net of probability connexions floating in open space'. As a result of this, he held, 'there will always be some blind posits on which the whole concatenation is based'.[35]

The upshot of my discussion of the regress of justification is that there is nothing wrong with our having some 'posits'. But there is no need to admit that they are 'blind', since they can be abandoned with the progress of inquiry, and their current justification accrues to them in virtue of how well we get along with the theory or system of beliefs of which they are part. Justification is not always, perhaps never is, a belief by belief affair such that for any belief, other than one which is self-justifying, there has to be some belief or beliefs which could be cited as its special justification.

Chisholm would not agree. He thinks that recognizing 'posits', as Reichenbach was prepared to do, involves 'letting go of the concept of justification'.[36] And this gives the game away, for it shows that the 'critique of cogency' and the 'Socratic' method by which it is conducted do not lead to the *discovery* that the ultimate justification for our various beliefs consists in their resting on a foundation of beliefs

[35] Hans Reichenbach, *Experience and Prediction* (Chicago: University of Chicago Press, 1938), p. 192.

[36] Chisholm, *Princeton Studies*, p. 268. Chisholm's view of the task of the epistemologist is very similar to that put forward by Pollock in 'What is an Epistemological Problem?'

which are self-justifying. As his reaction to Reichenbach shows, the concept of justification is understood in advance by Chisholm in such a way that no other result is possible, except perhaps scepticism should the enterprise fail. His approach to epistemology does not *lead to* the foundational view and does not yield any arguments for it independently of any that might be given for understanding 'justification' in the required way: it presupposes the foundational picture from the very beginning.

I take the point behind the objections of philosophers influenced by Dewey and Wittgenstein to be that they cannot see any reason to understand 'justification' in a way that leads to foundationalism, and so cannot see any point to the pursuit of traditional epistemology. Chisholm's account of the nature of epistemology does not answer such doubts since it presupposes the very notion of justification which these philosophers see no reason to accept. They are right not to accept it.

I have been suggesting that the rejection of this account of the nature of justification does not commit one to an alternative view about the essential nature of justification. The 'coherence theory' to which a no-foundations view of knowledge is committed simply in virtue of being a non-foundations view is trivial. If I had to offer an aphoristic statement of the essential nature of justification, I should probably say that being justified consists in doing or saying what your conscience and your society let you get away with. This is a vacuous remark, but it is meant to be. I have serious doubts whether there is much interesting to say about justification at this level of generality.

4. Meaning or Theory?

1. Introductory Remarks

Philosophers who agree that empirical knowledge rests on a foundation of epistemologically basic perceptual beliefs do not generally suppose that these beliefs exhaust what we know. Accordingly, they face the task of explaining how our foundational knowledge can serve to justify our claims to knowledge of non-basic fact. As we saw in chapter one, it is at this point that the threat of radical scepticism can become acute, for the sceptical argument purports to show that warranted inference from basic to non-basic knowledge is impossible. In this chapter, I shall consider the two main phenomenalist strategies for meeting the sceptical challenge. I shall argue that both are unsuccessful. To this extent, the sceptical position will be vindicated: but this will not be an argument in favour of scepticism, since I reject the foundational view of knowledge on which the sceptical argument depends. However, the fact that phenomenalistic theories which incorporate this view have no adequate defence against the challenge of scepticism provides a further reason for rejecting all such theories.

2. Analyticity and A Priori Knowledge

Classical phenomenalism proposed that reductive analyses of statements about the physical world could be given in terms of statements about sense-data. Many philosophers have come to feel that this programme was doomed from the start because the kind of analysis which phenomenalists in the classical mould had in mind is impossible in principle. No amount of information about how the physical world appears can *entail* that it must be some particular way rather than another. For any phenomenal story, it is possible to tell alternative stories about how things are in the physical world, all of which have identical experiential consequences. If all else fails, we can always imagine that we are brains kept alive in vats and that our perceptual experience is artificially stimulated and entirely delusive. This problem cannot be avoided by pointing out that phenomenalist translations will involve liberal use of conditionals saying how things would appear if . . .; for these will eventually have to be spelled out in phenomenal terms and, consequently, will themselves be as vulnerable to stories about brains in vats as any other purely phenomenal statements.

The truth of a finite set of phenomenal statements is not only not sufficient for the truth of a statement about the physical world, it is not even necessary.[1] Suppose that a pàrticular object is white: does this mean that it would appear white if I looked at it? Obviously not: the object would appear white only given certain physical and physiological conditions of perception. So the statement to the effect that the object in question is white will not entail a purely phenomenal statement but rather a conditional with some complex statement about physical conditions as antecedent. And the problem is perfectly general: if we ask whether this new statement entails any purely phenomenal statement, the same difficulty will arise all over again, and so on without end. In this respect, the argument to show that the truth of any purely phenomenal statement, no matter how complex, is never necessary for the truth of a statement

[1] See R. M. Chisholm, 'The Problem of Empiricism', *Journal of Philosophy*, Vol. XLV, no. 19 (September 1948).

about a physical object is perfectly analogous to the argument to show that the truth of such a statement is never sufficient either. The problem is not just, as Ayer once said, that 'one's references are vague in their application to phenomena',[2] it is that when we try to connect phenomenal statements with physical object statements then, no matter which way we want the entailment to go, we find that reference to physical conditions turns out to be ineliminable. If we try to eliminate it, we simply get involved in a regress.

I suppose that a hard-line defender of classical phenomenalism might object that, at least as far as the 'sufficiency' problem goes, this whole line of thought is not so much an *argument* against his theory as a claim, on the basis of an appeal to intuition, that it is obviously false. The 'argument' seems to require that various 'Cartesian' situations be clearly conceivable and, since the whole point of classical phenomenalism is to deny this, a defender of that theory might well feel that the objection is question-begging. Of course, anyone who took this line would still have to come to terms with the uncomfortable fact that not a single example of a phenomenalist translation has ever been given, a fact that is very strong evidence for the view that reductive analysis is in principle impossible. However, these days, we are more likely to encounter the claim that the relation between statements about how things appear and statements about how they really are is criteriological.[3] This relation is sometimes said to be neither inductive nor deductive. Criteriological relations hold in virtue of meaning and can be known to hold a priori. So the claim amounts to this: that it is analytic that if, for example, it looks to me as if there were

[2] A. J. Ayer, *The Foundations of Empirical Knowledge*, p. 242.

[3] See e.g. Pollock, 'The Structure of Epistemic Justification', *American Philosophical Quarterly Monograph Series*, No. 4. For an extensive bibliography on 'criteria' see W. G. Lycan, 'Noninductive Evidence: Recent Work on Wittgenstein's 'Criteria' '', *American Philosophical Quarterly*, Vol. 8 (1971), pp. 109–125.

something red before me, then there is reason for me to believe that there is something red before me.

This idea is sometimes defended by arguing that meaning is at least partially determined by justification conditions.[4] But this view of meaning is compatible with a no-foundations theory of knowledge. If we take the meaning of a belief to be determined at least in part by its inferential role in thought, then we can say that it is part of the meaning of perceptual beliefs that they function as grounds for inferences to beliefs about how things are in the physical world. But to say this is not to commit oneself to the view that there is such a thing as truth in virtue of meaning, where this is to be contrasted with truth in virtue of empirical fact.

From the standpoint of phenomenalism, the point of the appeal to the notion of analyticity is to explain how certain evidential connexions can be known to hold a priori or, alternatively, how they can be intrinsically credible. But some philosophers also bring in analyticity in order to explain how epistemologically basic beliefs can be intrinsically credible, as when they argue that it is an analytic, or conceptual, truth that a person's confident first-person perceptual beliefs are true most of the time.[5] In both cases the motivation is the same: to show how certain kinds of beliefs can be justified, and hence count as knowledge, without recourse to further matters of empirical fact. Recourse to such matters of fact, it is felt, would land us in some kind of regress of justification. This line of thought was discussed at some length in chapter three.

The idea that there are analytic truths on the one hand and synthetic truths on the other is bound up with a phenomenalistic view of knowledge at a very deep level. Quine has suggested that '. . . the unspoken

---

[4] Pollock, 'What Is an Epistemological Problem?' and 'Criteria and Our Knowledge of the Material World'.

[5] E. G. Sidney Shoemaker in *Self-Knowledge and Self-Identity* (Ithaca: Cornell University Press, 1963).

Weltanschauung from which the motivation and plausibility of a division of statements into analytic and synthetic arise' is '. . . a more or less attenuated holdover of phenomenalistic reductionism'.[6] Suppose that one thinks of knowledge as founded on a bedrock of hard data, the data recorded by basic phenomenal statements, from which all other kinds of statement are more or less remote. Then one can think of analytically true statements as standing at the limit of remoteness, the point at which the last traces of phenomenal or factual content disappear leaving only the bare formal structure of thought. It is a pleasing conception and essentially the same as the two-components view of knowledge which Lewis found to be presupposed by all traditional epistemologies, the two components being the sensuously given and the construction or interpretation imposed by the mind. If one is impressed by this view of knowledge, one can come to think that some statements might simply manipulate features of the construction, as it were, and thus be true independently of fact. As Lewis put it, 'Empirical truth . . . arises through conceptual inter-pretation of the given'. But there is also such a thing as conceptual truth: 'The concept gives rise to the a priori; all a priori truth is definitive, or explicative of concepts.'[7]

In treating the alleged distinction between analytic and synthetic truths as a theoretical distinction—i.e. a distinction which commits one to an explanatory claim—I am following Quine.[8] The claim in question is that there is such a thing as

[6] W. V. Quine, 'Mr. Strawson on Logical Theory', *Mind*, Vol. 62 (1953). Reprinted in Quine, *The Ways of Paradox and Other Essays* (New York: Random House, 1966). Quotation from p. 136 of this volume.

[7] Lewis, *Mind and the World Order*, p. 37.

[8] See his seminal papers 'Two Dogmas of Empiricism' in Quine, *From a Logical Point of View*, Revised edition (New York: Harper Torchbooks, 1961); and 'Truth by Convention', 'Carnap and Logical Truth' and 'Carnap's Views on Ontology', all in *The Ways of Paradox*. For an

truth solely in virtue of meaning, truth which is quite independent of empirical fact, and that this shows how there can be knowledge which is absolutely a priori. The main objection to the distinction is that this claim cannot be backed up.

Viewing the analytic/synthetic distinction in this light places strong constraints on what could be regarded as a defence of it. In particular, it would be obscurantism to claim to have defended the analytic/synthetic distinction if the distinction one has defended turns out to be incapable of performing any of the philosophical tasks which motivate the distinction in the first place. Philosophers who claim to accept the analytic/synthetic distinction while attempting to isolate the distinction from its traditional theoretical commitment are like modern theologians who claim to believe in the existence of God, though they do not believe in the existence of supernatural beings, old men in the sky, and so forth. Furthermore, the existence of analytic truths, in a full-blooded sense, cannot be established by an appeal to ordinary, commonsensical talk about meaning, or by an appeal to the fact that philosophers who feel at home with the distinction show substantial agreement as to the use of the expressions 'analytic' and 'synthetic' with respect to an open class of examples.[9] This would be like appealing to the linguistic intuitions of Calvinists in order to show that some people are saved and some damned. But, in point of fact, the alleged agreement has never existed. Most people could feel happy enough calling sentences like 'All bachelors are unmarried men' analytic. However, when we get to the interesting cases, the cases where the distinction is supposed

illuminating discussion of Quine's views, and one which clears away many of the misconceptions held by Quine's critics, see Gilbert Harman, 'Quine on Meaning and Existence' (Part 1), *Review of Metaphysics*, Vol. 21 (1967).

[9] H. P. Grice and P. F. Strawson, 'In Defence of a Dogma', *Philosophical Review*, Vol. 65 (1956), pp. 141-58.

to do important philosophical work, the consensus disappears.[10]

The view that knowledge has two separable components—that which is given to the senses and that which is imposed by the mind—has at least the appearance of offering some explanation of how analytic truth is possible. Unfortunately, as we saw in chapter two, the theory appears not to be coherent when one attempts to think it through.

A defender of phenomenalism needs an account of analyticity which shows how analytic truths can be a priori knowable. In *An Analysis of Knowledge and Valuation*, C. I. Lewis suggests that such truths reflect our intentions to use words in a particular way. 'Meaning postulates'—those truths which are 'explicative of concepts'—can be taken to implicitly define the terms they contain because we intend to use those terms in such a way that the postulates will come out true. There is no epistemological problem here because:

> . . . we know such truths by knowing what we mean; by grasping our own cognitive and intellectual intentions; by understanding what we commit ourselves to in adopting our own modes of classification and setting up criteria of them.[11]

[10] Anyone inclined to believe in the existence of the consensus should consult a variety of articles by philosophers at home with the analytic/synthetic distinction. A bewildering collection of statements have been candidates for being analytically true. It has been thought to be analytic that inductive reasons are good reasons, that every event has a cause, that 'visual space has three dimensions', that nothing can be both green and red all over: I could go on and on. But for every statement which some philosopher has declared to be analytic, there is almost certainly another philosopher, equally at home with distinction, who would dispute that statement's claim to analytic truth. Indeed, at the height of the distinction's popularity, a large slice of the philosophical debate of that time was given over to disputes over the purported analyticity of various philosophically important theses: for it was thought by many that distinctively philosophical theses were analytically true if true at all.

[11] C. I. Lewis, *An Analysis of Knowledge and Valuation* (LaSalle, Ill.: Open Court Publishing Co., 1946), p. 94.

For our purposes, this offers a plausible account of analytic truth. It makes analytic truth depend on our intentions and these are, arguably, known to us intuitively and a priori, if anything is. But, as Harman points out, the theory seems to add up to the contention that intending that a sentence be true can make it true: and how could this possibly happen?[12] It may indeed be true that we have to succeed in our intentions most of the time if we are to speak a language at all. But this applies equally to all sentences and does not single out a special class of analytic truths.

Consider the case of dreaming again. In the past, a person's repeated sincere denials upon waking that he had dreamt the night before constituted criterial evidence for his being a non-dreamer. This is the kind of evidential connexion which has been taken to be analytic and, no doubt, we did intend to use words in a way that respected the connexion. But discoveries which are clearly empirical have led to a refinement of the criterion. Our intentions notwithstanding, we held beliefs about this evidential relationship which were open to empirical disconfirmation, so the connexion could not have been analytic and the truth of the claim that repeated sincere denials in the appropriate circumstances show a person to be a non-dreamer depended on more than our intentions to use words in a certain way.

Lewis's theory is really a variant of the most popular account of analytic truth: that analytic truths are truths in virtue of linguistic convention.[13] There does seem to be a sense in which it is a matter of convention that particular words mean what they do. By 'glory', Humpty Dumpty

---

[12] Harman, *Thought*, ch. 1.

[13] An important statement of this position is to be found in H. Hahn, 'Logic, Mathematics, and Knowledge of Nature', in Ayer, *Logical Positivism*. See also Anthony Quinton, 'The A Priori and the Analytic', *Proceedings of the Aristotelian Society* (1963). Reprinted in P. F. Strawson (ed.), *Philosophical Logic* (London: Oxford University Press, 1967). References to this volume.

meant 'a nice knock-down argument'. The meanings of words depend on the conventions which govern their use. Some of these conventions will fix the meanings of certain words by specifying that certain sentences in which those words occur are to be counted true and that certain others are to be counted false. Thus the impossibility of falsification which attaches to analytic statements is not, in Quinton's words, 'a brute ontological fact; it is brought about by our refusal from the start to let any falsification occur.'[14] To change these conventions would be to change the meanings of at least some of the words involved, just as Humpty Dumpty changed the meaning of 'glory'.

It is sometimes said that this account of analytic truth cannot be correct because statements which report the existence of linguistic conventions must be empirical and synthetic. But this objection misses the point. The theory claims only that certain statements are true by convention, not that they report the existence of the conventions by virtue of which they are true.

Still, as Quine has shown,[15] the conventionalist account of analytic truth faces a fundamental problem. The problem is this: even if we grant that conventional assignments of truth and falsity determine meaning, from the fact that a statement is conventionally assigned the value 'true', it does not follow that it *is* true, let alone true by convention.

In chapter three, we saw that the appeal to truth in virtue of meaning seemed to offer an alternative to our simply accepting certain statements as 'postulates'. Suppose we introduce some new theoretical term 'T': we need to know something about what observable phenomena count in favour of the presence of Ts. That is, if 'T' is to have a use, we need some criteria, in a non-technical sense, for the presence of Ts. On pain of an infinite regress, not all such

14 Quinton, op. cit., p. 116.
15 See 'Truth by Convention'.

evidential relationships can have been established inductively. We might say, then, that the fact that observable phenomenon P counts as good evidence for the presence of Ts is one of the postulates of the theory of Ts. Proponents of criteria in the technical sense—i.e. the sense which presupposes a notion of analytic truth—are not content with this. They think that some such statements must be true in virtue of meaning. For example, many philosophers have held that it is true in virtue of the meaning of 'pain' that certain kinds of behaviour such as groaning, writhing on the ground and so on, count as good evidence for someone's being in pain. However, the notion used to explicate the concept of truth in virtue of meaning—that of conventionally counting some statements true—is indistinguishable from the notion of postulation, except by the fact that analytic statements, statements conventionally counted true, are thought to be immune from falsification. By assuming certain postulates of a theory to be true, we determine the meanings of the theory's primitive terms. As Quine points out, in whatever sense this is true of logic or mathematics, it is also true of theories in the other sciences.[16] But of course not every theory is true. 'Truth by virtue of convention' turns out to be 'truth according to one's postulates, or assumptions'. However, being assumed to be true is not the same as being true.[17]

[16] Ibid.

[17] It has been suggested to me that this argument misses two important points: (i) that something can be made (vacuously) true by its terms being assigned certain meanings and (ii) that by conventionally assigning the value 'true' to a sentence we can impose certain constraints on the meanings of its terms such that, as long as those constraints are not violated, it will be (vacuously) true. Thus the strongest objection to the phenomenalist's appeal to analytic truth is that if any statement is analytic, it is ipso facto uninformative and hence not a *truth* in the substantial sense required by his theory.

I cannot see that any of this is so. If the notion of analytic truth is countenanced at all then, since analyticity is held by its proponents to be hereditary with respect to deduction, there is no reason to suppose that

The upshot of all this is that the idea that certain statements are conventionally counted true cannot account for truth in virtue of meaning. For a statement can be conventionally counted true without its thereby being true. By the same token, the theory cannot show how it is possible to have absolutely a priori knowledge. One may know at the beginning of enquiry that a given statement is true according to one's assumptions or postulates, but one does not thereby know that it is true.

3. ANSWER OR CRITICISM?

A recent defender of phenomenalism, Jonathan Bennett,

there could not be unobvious analytic truths and that, consequently, such truths might be, in a perfectly straightforward sense, highly informative. This means, I think, that the claim that analytic truths are 'uninformative' or 'not substantial' cannot, upon examination, be distinguished from the claim that they are *analytic*. Clearly, there is nothing for a phenomenalist to worry about here.

In any case, the two points the argument is said to miss are really one. If we assign meanings to certain terms, presumably by setting forth certain definitions of 'meaning postulates', then this is just a matter of conventionally assigning certain sentences—those which state the postulates in question—the value 'true'. But now I would echo the point due to Quine and made in the text: that 'true by convention' cannot be distinguished from 'true according to one's conventions'. Since these conventions have no special immunity from revision in the light of further experience, it would be perverse to argue that truth according to one's conventions guarantees truth. The counter-claim that any such change of convention must involve change of meaning, besides invoking a concept of meaning which cannot be explained except by appealing to the disputed concept of analytic truth, is not easily made out in concrete cases, particularly when we have to deal with what Putnam calls 'law-cluster concepts'. Certainly, it cannot be made out in a way which points to the hard and fast distinction between change of meaning and change of belief which phenomenalism requires. But all I need to do in the present context of arguing against the use to which phenomenalism puts the idea of analytic truth is to undermine the view that 'conventional' truths have a specially privileged epistemic status and I think that the arguments given in the text are sufficient for this purpose.

claims that the theory is to be accepted because it provides an answer to or, alternatively, a criticism of the sceptically motivated question 'Is anything in the objective realm in any way as it appears to be?' which 'turns into' the question 'Is there really an objective realm at all?' The answer given is, of course, yes, 'on logical grounds', these being the connexion in virtue of meaning between the concepts of appearance and reality.[18]

It is not unusual for philosophers who appeal to meaning to claim that their strategy is one of criticizing and *dis*solving philosophical questions, rather than one of producing answers to them. However, I think that it is important at this stage in my argument to emphasize that there is a clear sense in which phenomenalism offers an answer to the sceptically motivated question rather than a criticism of the question itself. This is because phenomenalism shares with the sceptically motivated question the assumption that our knowledge of the physical world rests on a foundation of epistemologically basic perceptual knowledge. We may recall that the first step of the sceptical argument as reconstructed by Ayer is to insist that

> . . . we depend entirely on the premises for our knowledge of the conclusion. Thus it is maintained that we have no access to physical objects otherwise than through the contents of our sense-experiences.[19]

The point of Bennett's sceptically motivated question is to suggest that, since whatever knowledge we have of the physical world must rest ultimately on subjective data, there is no reason to suppose that we have any such knowledge. The general pattern of radically sceptical arguments is to throw out a challenge, given that knowledge rests on a

---

[18] Bennett, op. cit., p. 64.
[19] Ayer, *Problem of Knowledge*, p. 76.

restricted foundation, to show how knowledge of non-basic matters of fact is possible. Phenomenalism does not call in question this picture of our knowledge of the physical world. Rather it starts from the same foundational view of knowledge, but meets the sceptical challenge by insisting that certain statements which are true in virtue of meaning are at hand to licence inferences bridging the gap between beliefs about the physical world and the phenomenal data on which such beliefs, if justifiable, must ultimately rest.

This is why phenomenalism should be seen as answering rather than criticizing the sceptical question. It answers the question because it too incorporates the picture of justification which allows the argument implied by the sceptical question to get off the ground. A criticism of the question would consist in a critique of the idea that our knowledge of the physical world rests on a phenomenal foundation. But this is the fundamental idea which the phenomenalist shares with the sceptic.

4. THE HUMEAN THEORY

We have not dealt sympathetically with the phenomenalist's appeal to truth in virtue of meaning. However, it is possible to reject the appeal to analytic truth as a way of bridging the gap between basic and non-basic knowledge without giving up the idea that our knowledge of the physical world rests on a phenomenal foundation. The way to retain this idea is to argue that in talking about physical objects we are elaborating a theory with respect to the basic phenomenal evidence. The sceptical argument objects to the idea that the inference from this basic knowledge to a belief in the existence of physical objects could be inductive. A similar position is taken by those philosophers who think that at least some of the evidence-relations which back up inferences to beliefs about physical objects must be rooted in meaning.

But in both cases, it is assumed that induction by simple enumeration exhausts the field of possible inductive inference. In both the argument for radical scepticism, as presented in chapter one, and the argument in favour of analytic evidential connexions, we find the assumption that the evidence-relations linking 'perceptual' with 'higher-level' facts must be justified either inductively (by simple enumeration) or else analytically. In chapter three, I developed arguments to show that we should be dissatisfied with this dichotomy. So by my own standards, a version of phenomenalism which rejects this dichotomy deserves a hearing.

The alternative to the appeal to meaning, then, is to suggest that there is some form of inductive inference, other than induction by simple enumeration, by means of which the gap between basic and non-basic knowledge can be closed. The candidate which comes most naturally to mind is some form of the hypothetico-deductive method. However, I shall not bother with the details of this account since my argument will not depend on them. The basic idea is that the relation between phenomenal statements and statements about physical objects is like that between observation statements about macroscopic objects and statements about theoretical entities, such as electrons. Such entities are postulated to explain observable macro-events in the commonsense world of macro-objects. Similarly, this line of thought runs, the commonsense world of enduring, three-dimensional, publicly accessible objects is postulated to explain certain salient features of sense-experience: that is to say, it is epistemologically illuminating to see it in this light.[20]

---

[20] Pollock in 'Perceptual Knowledge' objects that a man could have justified beliefs about the physical world even if he had just had his sight restored by an operation and had never gone through this process of inferring the existence of physical objects as the best explanation of the course of experience. But not all advocates of the theory would want it to be taken genetically.

But how, one might ask, does this really differ from classical phenomenalism? Surely the theory of physical objects must contain 'meaning postulates' giving meaning to its theoretical terms, some of which must concern what phenomenal evidence counts in favour of the existence of what kinds of physical object. This is true, but the difference from classical phenomenalism lies in a rejection of the assumption that these 'meaning postulates' are acceptable because *true in virtue of meaning*. Rather their acceptability accrues to them in virtue of how well or how badly the theory of which they are a part helps us to get around within the realm of experience, and this is, of course, to deny that these other postulates are *meaning* postulates in any strong sense. On the other hand, we should not overestimate the difference between this view and classical phenomenalism. As we shall see, both theories share certain fundamental ideas, and one result of our examination of this modified view will be some additional insight into the shortcomings of the classical theory.

Perhaps the most famous advocate of such a modified view is Hume, although his discussion of these matters is notoriously confused.[21] Hume thought that the 'constancy and coherence' which we find in the order of our impressions provoke the mind into postulating the 'fiction' of continued and independent existences. In Hume's eyes, such an idea has to be a 'fiction' since it is neither given to sense, demonstrated from intuitive premises, nor established by causal reasoning (which he sees as enumerative induction), and these exhaust the sources of rational belief. Still, we can afford to be charitable and take Hume's talk of 'creating fictions' to be about what we should think of as elaborating a theory. So to mark its historical pedigree, I shall call the view we are presently considering 'the Humean theory'. One way to characterize the relation of this theory to classical

[21] See Hume, *A Treatise of Human Nature*, I.IV.2. My characterization of Hume's position is not strictly accurate.

phenomenalism would be as follows: physical objects are to be regarded as theoretical rather than logical constructions out of sense-data. However, the word 'construction' should not be taken too seriously since the general position I am calling 'the Humean theory' can quite readily be given a 'realistic' interpretation. In this form, the theory has sometimes been known as 'hypothetico-deductive realism'. The essence of the approach lies in its rejection of the idea that the inference to the belief in a physical world is grounded in analytic connexions in favour of the claim that in talking about physical objects we are elaborating a theory with respect to our experiential data, but its advocates are not bound to agree with Hume on the fictional status of the objects the theory introduces.

Of course, to be interesting, the view has to come to more than the claim that how things are in the physical world often explains how things look to particular perceivers. This is uncontroversial. The essential 'something more' which brands the theory as a variant of phenomenalism is the insistence on the epistemological priority of perceptual knowledge.

I think that the Humean view commands fairly widespread sympathy, even among philosophers not especially well-disposed towards classical phenomenalism. The idea that 'objectivity consists in there being a certain order in experience' is clearly a Humean view. This account of objectivity gives us an insight into another way in which a sense-datum, or pure-experience, language might be thought to be 'prior' to the language of physical things. As Ayer puts it

> . . . the 'sense-datum language' is, in a certain sense, more comprehensive than the 'physical-object language'. For whereas in every case in which it is possible to apply the physical object language it is also possible, at least in principle, to apply the sense-datum language, one can

conceive an order of experience to which the sense-datum
language would have application, but the physical-object
language would not.[22]

He quotes with approval a remark of Price to the effect that
'our visual and tactual data may have an eurrhythmic rather
than a thing-like order, arranging themselves as it were in
visible or tangible tunes.'[23] Putting on one side Ayer's
tendency to draw a sharp distinction between 'a language'
and 'a theory', we can say that he is putting forward the
claim that we can imagine circumstances in which the theory
of physical objects would be unacceptable.

There is no sharp distinction to be drawn between classical
phenomenalism and the Humean theory in this regard.
Whether we say that objects are logical constructions, or
whether we say they are theoretical constructions out of
sense-data, no version of phenomenalism will allow that any
old collection of sense-datum statements can add up to a
statement about the objective world. Or, to put it more
accurately from the standpoint of the Humean theory, not
every description of a possible sense-history is such that that
history can be described as sensory experience of an objective
world. Bennett's remark to the effect that phenomenalism
answers the sceptical question 'on logical grounds' can be
misleading. The 'logical' part of the answer draws attention
to the kind of empirical facts that are relevant—that is, facts
about experience—and shows how these are adequate to
justify our beliefs about the physical world. However, both
classical phenomenalism and the Humean theory go hand in
hand with a Humean account of objectivity, according to
which one's experience is experience of an objective world
only if it is in some way internally 'coherent'. But the inverse

[22] A. J. Ayer, 'The Terminology of Sense-Data' in Ayer, *Philosophical
Essays* (London: MacMillan, 1954). Quotation from p. 104.
[23] Ibid., p. 104. Price's remark comes from his review of Ayer's
Foundations, Mind, Vol. 50, pp. 280–293.

of this theory is that it is at least possible that one's experience should fail to be coherent in the required way.[24]

This can all seem very obvious, but actually it is very puzzling. As far as I can see, there is no such thing as a sense-history which *couldn't* be described as sensory experience of an objective world. The idea seems to be that our experience might just be a kaleidoscopic whirl of colours; but this is not an example of sense-experience which could not be described as experience of an objective world. To describe it as such, all we need are suitable hypotheses concerning the physical and physiological conditions of perception: think, for example, of what it would be like to watch an avant garde film while under the influence of some hallucinogenic drug. Under such conditions, one's experience would be strange indeed, and I think that this is the kind of thing that Ayer and Price have in mind. But it would not be experience which could not be described as experience of an objective world. Given suitable additional hypotheses, any experience can be so described.

Perhaps the point is meant to be somewhat weaker: that if all one's experience lacked the right kind of coherence, there would be no *use* for the conceptual framework of physical objects and perceivers.[25] If one's experience were always chaotic, there would be no way in which the use of concepts from the framework of objects and perceivers could help one to predict the future course of one's experience. Consequently, there would be no possibility of using such concepts to make justified assertions. Order within experience is a necessary condition for applying physical

---

[24] Strawson has tried to develop a Kantian argument against the possibility of our having what he calls 'the sense-datum experience'. See P. F. Strawson, *The Bounds of Sense* (London: Methuen, 1966). He is taken to task by Richard Rorty in 'Strawson's Objectivity Argument', *Review of Metaphysics*, Vol. 24 (1970).

[25] Something like this is suggested by Bennett in *Kant's Analytic* (Cambridge: Cambridge University Press, 1966). See especially ch. 3.

object concepts with either utility or justification. 'Coherent' experience, at the very minimum, must be experience about which it is possible to formulate inductively confirmable generalizations. Since, according to the view we are considering, 'coherent' experience is a precondition of its being possible to apply concepts from the conceptual framework of physical objects—or at least of there being any point to applying such concepts—the order to be found within experience must be describable without any help from concepts belonging to that framework. That is to say, it must be describable within what phenomenalists have sometimes called 'a pure-experience language', a language containing no descriptive terms except adjectives signifying sensory qualities. But if we needed this kind of experiential coherence before we could be justified in making any judgments involving physical-object concepts, we should never be justified in making such judgments: for, as I shall argue, if this is what it is for experience to be coherent, our experience is not coherent at all.

I have already argued that the existence of inductively confirmable generalizations, formulable within a purely experiential language—the 'coherence' of experience—is something to which classical phenomenalism, as well as the Humean theory, is committed. Another way to see this is to consider the traditional formulation of the classical theory: that objects are families of actual *and possible* sense-data.

The idea that we need to take into account possible as well as actual sense-data—in more explicitly linguistic terms, the idea that phenomenalist translations of statements about physical objects will contain many counterfactual conditionals stating how things would appear if . . . —is supposed to constitute modern phenomenalism's advance over Berkeley's idealism. Berkeley held the crude view that physical objects could be identified with collections of ideas. A succinct statement of his position is to be found in the opening paragraph of the *Principles*:

And as several of these (ideas) are observed to accompany each other, they come to be marked by one name, and so to be accounted one *thing*. Thus, for example, a certain colour, taste, smell, figure and consistence having been observed to go together, are accounted one distinct thing, signified by the name 'apple'; other collections of ideas constitute a stone, a tree, a book, and the like sensible things . . .[26]

The problem with this is that no object is continuously perceived. Berkeley, of course, was quite prepared to insist that the esse of sensible things like stones is percipi, but no modern phenomenalist would go along with him. Berkeley's claim to represent the vulgar view is not to be taken seriously. And there is the added problem that the 'ideas' which we would take to constitute an apple will vary with the physical and physiological conditions of perception: so even given a willingness to accept 'esse est percipi', Berkeley's simple analysis of talk about physical objects would be inadequate.

Modern phenomenalism meets these difficulties by substituting logical (or theoretical) constructions for Berkeley's simple collections. Bennett, who is concerned to point out the advantages of phenomenalism over the Berkeleian theory puts the point this way:

Phenomenalism says that any statement about the objective realm has a meaning which could be expressed in some set (not necessarily a conjunction) of statements about sense-data, and it adds that any such set will be long and complex and will contain members of the form 'If it were the case that . . ., then such and such sense-data would be had.' One short way of saying that any objectivity-statement is equivalent to a set of statements,

---

[26] Berkeley, *The Principles of Human Knowledge*, section 1.

including counterfactual conditionals, about sense-data, is to say that *Objects are logical constructions out of sense-data.*[27]

How are we to understand the idea that the family of sense-data constituting a given physical object will contain possible as well as actual sense-data? In other words, what sorts of things will fill the blanks in the members of the form 'If it were the case that . . ., then such and such sense-data would be had'? Objects are not, in general, continuously perceived; and the appearances they present vary with changes in the physical and physiological conditions of perception: this is why the need arose to incorporate such conditionals into phenomenalist translations in the first place. But if the conditionals are to do what is expected of them, then surely the way to understand them (and hence the notion of possible sense-data) is to take them to be statements specifying how things would appear if there were a perceiver present, or if the physical and physiological conditions of perception were to be thus and so. However, it is clear that no proponent of classical phenomenalism can adopt this interpretation of the relevant counterfactual conditionals. Phenomenalism states that all statements about physical objects have a meaning which could be expressed by some complex set of statements about sense-data. So if the counterfactual members of such a set are formulated as suggested above, the statements about perceivers, physical objects and conditions of perception contained in their protases will themselves need to be spelled out in sense-datum terms: and now we are threatened with a vicious regress. The phenomenalist translations may even become circular: for example, through statements about physical and physiological conditions of perception (statements about the perceptual apparatus perhaps) being explicated in terms of

[27] Bennett, *Locke, Berkeley, Hume*, p. 136.

conditional sense-datum statements which involve essential reference to those very same conditions.

To avoid this unpleasant consequence, a defender of classical phenomenalism must hold that the possible sense-data which go into the family which constitutes a given particular physical object must be specifiable without any appeal to the conceptual framework of perceivers and physical objects. After all, this is just what is to be analysed, and phenomenalism is as committed to constructing the self as it is to constructing the external world.[28] But, to revert to the linguistic mode, the important fact is this: that the counterfactual conditionals of which classical phenomenalism makes so much must be grounded in inductively confirmable generalizations formulable within a purely experiential language. The ultimate facts must be facts about *actual* sense-data. When Hylas tries to introduce facts about the brain in their discussion, Philonous reminds him that 'The brain . . . you speak of, being a sensible thing, exists only in the mind',[29] which is just what a consistent phenomenalist should say.

The upshot of all this is that classical phenomenalism and the Humean theory are committed to the same basic idea: that there are inductively confirmable generalizations about the course of experience formulable without any help from the language of physical objects and perceivers. But the most cursory examination of Hume's own writings reveals that he fails dismally in his attempt to indicate what these might be. His achievement is supposed to be to have called our attention to the constancy and coherence in the order of our impressions and to have pointed out that these are the characteristics of experience upon which the inference to a belief in an objective world depends. But what does Humean 'constancy' amount to?

[28] Hume was right. See also Ayer, 'Phenomenalism', ch. 6, in *Philosophical Essays*.
[29] Berkeley, *Three Dialogues Between Hylas and Philonous*.

After a little examination, we shall find, that all those objects, to which we attribute a continued existence, have a peculiar *constancy,* which distinguishes them from the impressions, whose existence depends upon our perception. Those mountains, and houses, and trees, which lie at present under my eye, have always appeared to me in the same order; and when I lose sight of them by shutting my eyes or turning my head, I soon after find them return upon me without the least alteration.[30]

Hume recognizes that this constancy is not perfect, and this is where 'coherence' becomes important:

Bodies often change their position and qualities, and after a little absence or interruption may become hardly knowable. But here 'tis observable, that even in these changes they preserve a *coherence,* and have a regular dependence on each other . . .

Thus:

When I return to my chamber after an hour's absence, I find not my fire in the same situation, in which I left it: But then I am accustomed in other instances to see a like alteration produced in a like time, whether I am present or absent, near or remote. This coherence, therefore, in their changes is one of the characteristics of external objects, as well as their constancy.[31]

Earlier in the discussion, we saw that the way to react to the inadequacies of Berkeleian idealism is to admit that phenomenalist translations of statements about physical objects will contain many counterfactual conditionals saying how things would appear if . . . The problem with this was

[30] Hume, *Treatise*, I.IV.2. p. 194 in the Selby-Bigge edition.
[31] Ibid., p. 195.

that, if the counterfactual conditionals are to do what is required of them, it looks as if they have to say how things would appear if there were a perceiver present, or if the conditions of perception were to be thus and so. We also concluded that it would be an error for an advocate of phenomenalism to see the relevant conditionals in this light. The passages quoted above strongly suggest that Hume is guilty of a very similar mistake. Like the modern phenomenalist, he needs there to be an order within experience describable without any help from the conceptual framework of physical objects and perceivers. But instead of this, he calls our attention to certain *dependent* experiential regularities. Given certain facts about the physical situation, there is a discernible regularity in the way that physical objects appear to us. However, this is not the kind of order within experience his theory needs.

Even the most sympathetic commentators would admit that Hume writes rather loosely. What we must do is to reconstruct constancy and coherence as features of sets of impressions.[32] After all, Hume's loose presentation of his theory is in part a consequence of his feeling free to talk indifferently of objects or impressions. Hume gives warning that, in order to accommodate himself to the notions of the vulgar, he will understand by 'object' and 'perception', 'what any common man means by a hat, or shoe, or stone, *or any other impression conveyed to him by his senses*' (my emphasis). He even seems to think that the inference to a belief in an objective world is an inference to the belief that one's impressions continue to exist even when not present to the mind.

Bennett reconstructs Hume's view as follows:

Coherence is just orderliness: a 'coherent' set of

---

[32] See H. H. Price, *Hume's Theory of the External World* (Oxford: Clarendon Press, 1940). Also, Bennett, *Locke, Berkeley, Hume*, ch. 13.

impressions is one conforming to some generalisation to which many other sets also conform. Constancy is a special case of coherence: a 'constant' set of impressions is one conforming to the generalisation 'Each member of the set is exactly like the preceding member.'[33]

But here is the rub: once we purify Hume's presentation of his theory and reconstruct constancy and coherence as features of sets of impressions—features which presuppose the existence of inductively confirmable generalisations formulable in a purely experiential language—then there is no reason to suppose that experience is 'coherent' in the way that his theory requires.

It is only because Hume helps himself freely to concepts from the language of physical objects and perceivers that the kind of theory he advocates has the slightest plausibility. His talk of the 'coherence' of experience has a measure of intuitive plausibility just because he is able to direct our attention to all kinds of dependent regularities to be found in experience: regularities, that is, which are dependent on, or restricted to, certain objective conditions of perception. Hume's mistake, and that of his followers, is of a piece with that committed by phenomenalists who think that their translations of statements about physical objects can contain counterfactual conditionals stating how things would appear if there were to be a perceiver present, or if such and such conditions of perception were to obtain. It is all very well for Hume to call attention to the constancy of the appearance of the mountains, or the coherence of the appearances presented by his fire. But suppose we stick to yellow-orange sense-data (the kind we may suppose fires to produce under normal perceptual conditions). Maybe we have noticed that the occurrence of such sense-data has been correlated with certain striped sense-data (those produced by the wallpaper

[33] Bennett, *Locke, Berkeley, Hume*, p. 323.

on the wall next to the fireplace). But if the conditions of illumination change, if we visit a friend's house and look into his fire, if we close our eyes for a moment while dozing in front of the fire, if we have the room redecorated—in short, if any one of countless ordinary events takes place—the generalization linking the occurrence of yellowy-orange flickering sense-data to the occurrence of striped sense-data will be disconfirmed. The problem is that our sense-experience reflects every idiosyncratic feature of the physical and physiological environment in which we happen to live.[34] If we are not allowed to impose any restrictions on the conditions of perception, but are limited instead to the resources of a purely experiential language, we will never be able to formulate any inductively confirmable generalizations about the course of experience. Hume notes that the mountains, houses and trees have always appeared to him in a constant order: but suppose we try to restate this point in terms of purple patches, green patches, and so on. His argument evaporates. The Humean theory—that in talking about physical objects we are elaborating a theory with respect to our experiential data—cannot be correct. The reason for this is that the predicates of a purely experiential language would not be projectible.[35] And if the epistemological order which lies at the heart of the Humean view is to be respected, an appeal to the conceptual framework of physical objects for the purpose of demonstrating order at the level of experience cannot be

---

[34] As Hume well knew:

'We remark a connexion betwixt two kinds of objects in their past appearance to the senses, but are not able to observe this connexion to be perfectly constant, since the turning about of our head or the shutting of our eyes is able to break it.'

(*Treatise*, pp. 197-198). But he did not appreciate how serious a difficulty this admission raises.

[35] I think that this is the point Sellars wants to make via his claim that 'phenomenal' generalisations would be 'essentially autobiographical'. See *Science, Perception and Reality*, ch. 3, sect. 3.

tolerated, just as an attempt to specify the possible sense-data belonging to the family constituting a given object by invoking counterfactual conditionals stating how things would appear if the physical and physiological conditions were thus and so cannot be tolerated within the confines of classical phenomenalism.

How might a defender of the Humean theory reply to this? Clearly, the argument counts strongly against variants of Ayer's 'scientific approach', for example the view once canvassed by Russell that we infer the existence of physical objects as the simplest explanation of the orderliness of our sensory experience. The theory of physical objects is thought to be elaborated in response to certain features of our primary experiential data, the features also emphasized by advocates of the view that objectivity consists in there being a certain order in experience, experiential constancy and coherence. But if constancy and coherence cannot, in Bennett's phrase, be 'reconstructed as features of sets of impressions', the grounds for the inference, the data which the theory of physical objects is to explain, simply disappear.[36] However, it might be claimed that Hume's own account of the inference to a belief in a world of persisting objects is not vulnerable to this objection. Hume is himself at pains to point out that our experience is far from completely coherent, and it is in response to this *imperfect* coherence

---

[36] It might be thought that this objection presupposes too strong a distinction between observation and theory: does it matter if the experiential data cannot be described in a way that is completely neutral with respect to the theory of physical objects? The answer is that it matters to an advocate of the Humean theory or any other theory of knowledge which is, in my broad sense, phenomenalist. To give up the hard-and-fast distinction between theory and observation and to allow that we may need to help ourselves to physical object talk to be able even to describe the relevant features of the sensory data is to abandon the commitment to the concept of a strict epistemological order which gives the Humean theory, and all other phenomenalist theories, their philosophical point. The idea that there is a rigid observation/theory distinction is just another aspect of the phenomenalist outlook in epistemology.

that we imaginatively construct a world in which there is far more constancy and coherence than we could hope to find in the world of impressions alone. Thus:

> Objects have a certain coherence even as they appear to our senses; but this coherence is much greater and more uniform if we suppose the objects to have a continued existence.[37]

But this will not do. Even in its 'imaginative supplementation' version, the Humean theory still requires a good measure of constancy and coherence within unsupplemented experience, and I have argued that, when 'constancy' and 'coherence' are properly understood—that is, understood to imply a commitment to the existence of inductively confirmable generalizations formulable within a purely experiential language—there is no reason to suppose that experience is coherent *at all* and every reason to suppose that it is not. So it will not do to argue in reply that experience is only more or less coherent. To locate any order within experience we need to be able to place some restrictions on the relevant conditions of perception. It is no accident that whenever Hume offers an example of constancy or coherence, even imperfect constancy or coherence, he talks about how objects have appeared to him. Indeed, I might add that it is far from clear that Hume's presentation of his 'imaginative supplementation' theory is even consistent. He writes:

> There is scarce a moment of my life, wherein . . . I have not occasion to suppose the continued existence of objects, in order to connect their past and present appearances, and give them such an union with each other, as I have found by experience to be suitable to their

---

[37] Hume, *Treatise*, p. 198.

particular natures and circumstances.[38]

But could Hume find by experience certain regularities to be 'suitable to their natures' if there is 'scarce a moment' when he is not obliged to bring in the supposition of continued existence to fill in the gaps?[39]

There are very few knock-down arguments in philosophy, and I do not claim to have given one. An advocate of the Humean theory can always reply that the antecedents of any conditionals formulated in purely experiential terms would have to be *very* complicated in order to avoid precipitous disconfirmation. But it seems to me that to adopt this line of defence would be to decide to hold on to the theory at all costs. Certainly, the theory's appeal vanishes once the force of the objection is recognized. The original claim was that the commonsense world of objects and perceivers is postulated in response to certain obvious features of sense-experience: now we find that the order that exists within sense-experience is complex indeed, so complex in fact that we no longer have any guarantee that such order is there to be found.

This is the point at which it becomes relevant to ask why anyone should feel that the theory needs to be defended at all costs. Why, that is, does *some* version of phenomenalism have to be correct? If the argument of chapter three was successful, it doesn't.

---

[38] Ibid., p. 197.

[39] Hume finds it impossible to square this process of imaginative supplementation with the theory of belief developed in the course of his discussion of inductive inference. This latter theory implies that it is impossible both 'that any habit should ever be acquired otherwise than by the regular succession of . . . perceptions' and 'that any habit should ever succeed that degree of regularity' (*Treatise,* p. 197, Selby-Bigge edition). This wouldn't matter to Hume if we just thought of the physical world as an agreeable fantasy. Unfortunately, we believe in its existence.

5. Basic Propositions

1. SENSE-DATA RECONSIDERED

I suggested at the beginning of chapter three that the basic idea behind all phenomenalisms is that our knowledge of the physical world rests on a foundation of perceptual knowledge, in some sense of 'perceptual'. A second idea, distinctive of mainstream phenomenalist epistemologies, is that our (inferential) knowledge of the physical world is anchored to its foundation by various truths which hold in virtue of meaning and independently of fact. We did not deal sympathetically with the appeal to truth in virtue of meaning. This is one reason why it was important to consider the Humean theory: for this theory promised to show us how to retain an essentially phenomenalist theory of knowledge without acquiring a commitment to defend the notion of analytic truth. Having rejected the Humean theory, it is time to pick up again the critique, begun in chapter three, of the idea that our knowledge of the physical world rests on a foundation of epistemologically basic perceptual beliefs.

Traditionally, phenomenalists have founded empirical knowledge on the givenness of sense-data. In chapter two, we examined a number of problems involved in this appeal to 'the given'. But it could be argued that this earlier criticism is effective only against the traditional conception of sense-data and does not constitute adequate grounds for rejecting anything which might legitimately be called a version of the sense-datum theory. Bennett, in a recent defence of phenomenalism, argues that confusion over the ontological status of sense-data has been responsible, in large measure, for bringing traditional phenomenalism into disrepute.[1] Such confusion has been the source of various 'mildly lunatic conundrums' which nobody would ever have taken seriously had they not seemed inextricably bound up with matters of clear philosophical importance. Thus philosophers have wasted much time and energy worrying about whether sense-data can exist unperceived, whether they are literally on the surface of physical objects, and so on. There are also problems arising out of their being *private* particulars. The idea that our knowledge of the public physical world is an inferential construction based ultimately on private experiential data has been heavily criticized in recent years. Philosophers influenced by Wittgenstein have argued that 'inner processes stand in need of outward criteria' and that, consequently, the 'pure experience language' which phenomenalists have taken to record our ultimate phenomenal data is not a possible language at all.[2] A similar point is made by Strawson: he argues that one could not have a language which spoke only of 'sensations' or 'experiences' because a minimum condition for knowing what an experience is is that one know what a person is. This knowledge requires the ability to pick out persons, which in turn

---

[1] Jonathan Bennett, *Locke, Berkeley, Hume.* See especially pp. 31-35.

[2] A classic presentation of the Wittgensteinian view is given by Norman Malcolm in *The Philosophical Review*, Vol. 63 (1954), pp. 530-559. Whether Malcolm gives an accurate account of Wittgenstein's views, and whether the arguments are any good, are controversial questions. A useful collection of papers on this topic can be found in *Wittgenstein—The Philosophical Investigations*, ed. George Pitcher (New York: Anchor Books, 1966). An admirably clear discussion of the issues raised by Wittgenstein's 'private-language argument' is given by John Turk Saunders and Donald F. Henze in their book *The Private-Language Problem* (New York: Random House, 1967). Most important of all, see Ludwig Wittgenstein, *Philosophical Investigations*, trans. G. E. M. Anscombe (New York: MacMillan, 1953).

presupposes the ability to talk about physical objects.[3]

The central idea behind these anti-phenomenalist arguments is a rejection of the notion that experience is 'self-luminescent', that one can know all about one's experiences simply by having them. This in turn means giving up the idea that the terms in a phenomenal language could be given meaning simply by acts of private ostensive definition. All this fits in well with the doubts about the alleged 'givenness' of sense-data, which I have expressed throughout my argument. However, when these critics of phenomenalism go on to claim that, in order for talk of private objects like sensations to be possible, there must be 'logically adequate' behavioural criteria, it looks as though we shall have to part company: for they are saying that talk of pain, for example, is possible because it is *analytically true* that certain kinds of behaviour constitute good or even conclusive evidence for someone's being in pain. But Rorty argues that this appeal to analytic truth is quite unnecessary:

What then does it come to . . . to say that the relation between sensations and behaviour is non-contingent? Merely, I think, the claim that before sensations can be talked of, certain pieces of behaviour must be capable of being talked of as well, and that some statement about the latter being evidence for the former must be accepted by the speaker. But this is not to say that the statement which asserts that such-and-such behaviour is evidence for another's having such and such a sensation must itself assert a necessary relationship. Some evidential relationship must necessarily exist, but it need not be a relationship which makes any piece of behaviour guarantee the existence of any particular experience. In other words: It is necessary for knowledge or talk of sensations to exist that the knower or talker use behavior

[3] P. F. Strawson, *Individuals* (London, Methuen, 1959), ch. 3.

as evidence for sensations, but he need not take any such behavior as *conclusive* evidence for sensations. The claim that the private-language argument, or Strawson's argument in *Individuals,* shows that statements about behaviour must be 'logically adequate criteria' for statements about sensations is a confusion of modalities.[4]

Rorty calls his purified form of the kind of argument advanced by Strawson (and perhaps Wittgenstein) 'the parasitism argument'. It is an argument which purports to show what we must be able to talk about, or have knowledge of, if we are to be able to talk or have knowledge of something else.

Now Bennett argues that, although disenchantment with various puzzles arising out of the traditional conception of the sense-datum as a peculiar kind of private object has led to a widespread rejection of phenomenalism, this rejection has been premature. All such puzzles can be visibly dissolved by a correct parsing of the sentence 'He has a Ø sense-datum.' He offers two alternatives:

(1) It is with him as though he were perceiving a . . .
(2) He is sensorily affected in the way he usually is when he perceives a . . .[5]

Bennett here presents a version of a view which has become popular in recent years and which we may call the *adverbial theory*. Another notable proponent, who is also a

[4] Richard Rorty, 'Criteria and Necessity' NOUS 1973. See also his papers 'Strawson's Objectivity Argument', *The Review of Metaphysics*, Vol. 24, No. 2 (December 1970); and 'Verificationism and Transcendental Arguments', NOUS, Vol. 5, No. 1. In the latter paper, Rorty is responding to arguments put forward by Judith Thomson in 'Private Languages', *American Philosophical Quarterly*, Vol. 1 (1964), and by Barry Stroud, 'Transcendental Arguments', *The Journal of Philosophy*, Vol. 55 (1968).

[5] Bennett, op. cit., p. 33.

phenomenalist by my standards, is Chisholm.[6] He would agree with Bennett that beliefs about appearances provide a foundation for our beliefs about the physical world (though he recognizes other 'sources' of knowledge as well) and he would also agree that we must be careful how we construe statements about appearances. We should not take them to refer to a special kind of particular, an appearance. Rather the most perspicuous way of expressing the content of beliefs about 'appearances' is through sentences like 'I am appeared to redly'. Beliefs about appearances are really beliefs about *how one is appeared to.*

Bennett calls his account of sense-data 'the anti-reification thesis'. He clarifies his strategy by first displaying it in a less controversial context. He considers the question 'Are there such things as moods?' His answer is, on the one hand, 'Of course there are moods.' But, on the other hand, it is wrong to reify them. Two reasons are given for this:

> . . . the only intelligible statements about moods are statements which may be negative, general, conditional, etc., about people's being *in* moods.

> . . . any statement about a person's being in a mood is equivalent to an explicitly non-relational statement about that person.[7]

For example, 'He is in a good mood' according to Bennett is equivalent to 'He is cheerful and friendly'. Furthermore, although we can say of a mood whose mood it was and how long it lasted, we cannot ask, e.g., whether it was literally blacker than pitch, or indulge in too much speculation about the relation of in-ness which a man has to his mood:

> Because a mood's existing is its having this one unique

---

[6] For a recent presentation of his views, see R. M. Chisholm, *Theory of Knowledge.*

[7] Bennett, op. cit., p. 32.

'relation' to some person, the 'relation' is not a relation at all.[8]

One might have expected Bennett to claim that, strictly speaking, there are no such things as moods: for he has argued in effect that the intelligible content of any statement containing apparent reference to a mood can be completely captured by some statement referring only to a person, the apparent reference to the mood being always eliminable. But he does not say this: he claims only that moods are 'radically un-thing-like'. Moods are not things, they are emotional states. Similar considerations show that sense-data are not things either; they are sensory states:

> . . . any statement about someone's having a sense-datum is equivalent to an explicitly non-relational statement about that person, attributing to him a certain sensory state, saying how he sensorily is.[9]

I do not know whether Bennett's distinction between being 'thing-like' and being 'state-like'[10] can be made any clearer than Bennett makes it. For reasons which will become apparent, I do not think it matters much one way or the other. The intuitive appeal of the adverbial theory lies in its offering an escape from what Austin called 'the ontology of the sensible manifold' by explicating talk about sense-data, appearances, and so on in terms of talk about persons and their sensory states.

At this point, we should remind ourselves of the philosophical task which a phenomenalist theory of knowledge is designed to perform: that is, to rebut the argument for radical scepticism. As Bennett puts it, the reason for accepting phenomenalism is that it provides an answer to the sceptically motivated question 'Is anything in

8 Ibid., p. 33.
9 Ibid., p. 33.
10 This is not a phrase Bennett uses.

the objective realm in any way as it appears to be?' which 'turns into' the question 'Is there really an objective realm at all?' The argument implied by the question is that, since our knowledge of 'reality' must be founded on what we know about appearances, there is no reason to suppose that we have any such knowledge. A defender of phenomenalism will accept the premise but deny the conclusion, for he will argue that the gap can be bridged, either by some connexions which hold in virtue of meaning, or by some form of theoretical inference. However, adopting an account of 'appearances' along the lines suggested by Bennett requires a corresponding reconstruction of the distinction between 'appearance' and 'reality' in terms of which the sceptical question is posed. Accordingly, in the spirit of his anti-reification thesis, Bennett uses 'appearance/reality' to refer to the distinction which has 'facts about sensory states on one side of it and everything else on the other'.[11] But if 'everything else' is supposed to add up to facts about 'the objective realm', as the formulation of the sceptical question suggests that it must, then this is not the distinction he wants. For facts about sensory states are themselves facts about the objective realm. They must be since, according to the anti-reification thesis, they are facts about people, and people are among the constituents of the objective realm.

It is no use replying that, if some version of phenomenalism is true, then statements about people will be analysable into or fully justifiable on the basis of statements about appearances. This reply appeals to a traditional understanding of phenomenalism which accepts talk about appearances, the ontology of the sensible manifold, as primitive. But the objection is directed against the idea that phenomenalism can be made more respectable if it is made to incorporate an adverbial analysis of such talk.

Bennett's distinction, then, turns, out to be between some

[11] Bennett, op. cit., p. 64.

facts about the objective realm, namely those having to do with people being in sensory states, and all other such facts. Phenomenalism, in Bennett's view the theory which spells out the logical link between the concepts of appearance and reality, must now be seen as postulating analytic connexions between statements about the objective realm at large and statements which, although alleged to be epistemologically privileged, are just as much statements about the objective realm. Thus revised, the theory cannot answer the question 'Is anything in the objective realm in any way as it appears to be?' or the question 'Is there really an objective realm at all?' Phenomenalism revised in accordance with the adverbial theory answers these questions by referring the sceptic to further facts about the objective realm. Thus, if there were a serious question to beg, the theory would beg it.

Difficulties like this produce a tendency, which we shall encounter again, for latter-day phenomenalists to lapse into more traditional ways of thinking when putting their theory to work or when under pressure to explain how it could work. Recall Bennett's treatment of Locke's attempt to defend our belief that some of our perceptions represent 'real things external to the mind' by arguing that

> It is plain that those perceptions are produced in us by exterior causes affecting our senses: because those that want the organs of any sense can never have the ideas belonging to that sense produced in their minds.[12]

Commenting on this passage, Bennett remarks that it is question-begging since it has 'a premise about sense-organs' and sense-organs are among the 'things without us' whose reality is in question.[13] This kind of objection would not be so readily available if he were taking his own account of

---

[12] Locke, *Essay*, IV.XI.4. Quoted by Bennett, op. cit., p. 66.
[13] Bennett, op. cit., p. 66.

talk about appearances seriously. His own version of phenomenalism, revised in accordance with the anti-reification thesis, is similarly question-begging.

It might be said that my line of criticism misses the point. For this revised phenomenalism claims only that when someone knows a sense-datum statement to be true, what he knows to be true is a statement about—i.e. a statement in fact involving a reference to—a person. Granted, persons are among the constituents of the objective world, but this is not asserted by the sense-datum statement, and knowledge of this fact is not presupposed by my knowing, say, that I am appeared to redly. The indexical 'I' picks out its referent demonstratively: knowledge of special facts about the referent is not required.

To this I am inclined to reply that there is no reason to suppose that, in the absence of the usual background knowledge of how to identify and reidentify people, the word 'I' could be used to refer at all. The primary function of 'I' is to call attention to the speaker. Thus knowing how to use the word entails knowing a good deal about the objective world, and this is what seems to make the 'I am appeared to . . .' locution unsuitable for the expression of a phenomenalist's epistemologically basic beliefs. It is not for nothing that many traditional phenomenalists have thought that the construction of the self and the construction of the physical world are tasks to be performed together.

Of course, there have been theories designed to free our talk of sensory states and the like from their dependence on our knowledge of persons and the objective world to which they belong. From time to time, Russell, who was worried about his use of 'I' to refer to 'a more or less permanent person', toyed with the idea that the self is an introspectively given particular. But the idea is not very appealing, least of all to anyone who has any sympathy with the considerations which motivate the anti-reification thesis. For the result of such a move would be to swap some lunatic conundrums about sense-data for some equally lunatic conundrums about the self.

This shows, I think, how relatively unimportant is the 'adverbializing' aspect of Bennett's account of sense-data. There would be little to gain from the insistence that sense-data or appearances should be construed as talk about states rather than things, if the things of which they are states were taken to be Cartesian egos. The idea that talk about sense-data or appearances should be construed as talk about people and their sensory states seems philosophically illuminating just so long as we stick to our intuitive conception of what people are: among other things, embodied occupants of the physical world whose behaviour constitutes evidence for their mental states. In other words, the plausibility of the anti-reification thesis springs from its conceding just the point which Rorty hopes to establish by means of his 'parasitism' argument.[14] This argument, we may recall, purports to show what we must be able to talk about or have knowledge of if we are to talk or have knowledge of something else. In particular, we must already be able to talk of physical objects and persons if we are to talk of 'appearances'. This is just what Bennett's anti-reificationist analysis of appearance-talk in terms of talk about people and their sensory states implies.

I have been arguing that phenomenalism cannot be made more appealing by analysing sense-datum statements along the lines suggested by Bennett's anti-reification thesis. I think, however, that some suspicion must remain that the argument works best against the project of combining such an analysis of sense-datum statements with classical phenomenalism, or with the Humean theory. Because classical phenomenalism claims that all statements about the objective world are fully analysable into complex statements

[14] Thus Bennett: 'I . . . agree with those who say that if we are to describe sense-data in publicly intelligible ways we must avail ourselves of physical-object language.' Op. cit., p. 34.

about sense-data, an advocate of the theory cannot consistently adopt an analysis of sense-datum statements which invokes concepts appropriate to the kinds of statement which his theory is meant to analyse. And there is the added danger that such an analysis of sense-datum statements may serve to mask some of the fundamental difficulties which classical phenomenalism has to face. We saw in chapter four that although any phenomenalist analysis of a statement about the physical world must rely heavily on statements about how things would appear if such and such were the case, the protases of such conditionals cannot be formulated straightforwardly in terms of the physical and physiological conditions of perception. An analysis of sense-datum statements which makes illicit use of concepts from our full-blooded view of the world, namely those having to do with persons and their sensory states, obscures this crucial problem and thereby lends to the analytical programme of classical phenomenalism an additional, though altogether specious, degree of plausibility.

The project of combining a Bennett-like analysis of sense-datum statements with the Humean theory faces a similar difficulty. This theory claims that physical-object concepts are introduced into the language as part of a theory which helps us get around our 'experience'. But the Humean view does suppose that the facts about our experience can be stated without appeal to the theory introduced in response to those facts. Our sense-datum talk, according to this view, does not presuppose an ability to wield concepts belonging to the physical-object language.

But what if we embrace some weaker version of phenomenalism, perhaps one to the effect that there is a 'logical link' between the concepts of appearance and reality, that sense-datum statements provide 'logical reasons' or 'criterial evidence' for the truth of statements about the external world. If we do not insist on either the reductive programme of classical phenomenalism or the constructive programme of the Humean theory, why should the fact, if it is a fact, that talk of sense-data and the like is 'parasitic' upon the conceptual scheme of persons and physical things, preclude sense-datum statements from fulfilling a special role, namely a foundational (epistemologically basic) role, in whatever justification we have for our beliefs about the world?

A natural reply would be to argue that, if our talk of sense-data or appearances is parasitic on our conceptual scheme of persons and physical objects, in the sense that one could not be said to understand or know to be true any sense-datum statement unless one *already knew* a good deal about the objective world, then surely our knowledge of that world cannot rest on a foundation of prior knowledge of appearances. This seems to be the argument in the minds of philosophers who use parasitism arguments to develop anti-phenomenalist and anti-sceptical positions. However, this argument alone is not conclusive. A defender of a weakened phenomenalism can reply that, in assigning a foundational role to certain statements, he is interested in their *epistemological* and not their ·genetic priority and that, consequently, he can concede the point about 'parasitism' without damage to his position. In explaining what a sense-datum statement is, he may say, we have no choice but to appeal to our knowledge of such things as persons, sensory states, and so on; and it is true that such concepts are an integral part of our 'physical-object' language. But to admit this is not to commit oneself to denying the basic tenets of phenomenalism: that certain first-person perceptual reports, call them sense-datum statements, are known in a special way and are thus able to fulfil a special role—a foundational role—in justifying our beliefs about the physical world.

To be effective as an anti-phenomenalist argument, the parasitism argument must impute to the defender of phenomenalism the view that statements expressing epistemologically basic beliefs could be known to be true without anything else being known. The argument gives voice to a reasonable doubt as to whether there could be such statements. In the background is a view of meaning which reflects a reluctance to talk of meaning in isolation from general schemes for construing utterances and attributing beliefs. The idea is that we will take an utterance to be an expression of a particular perceptual belief only if the speaker accepts the sentence in circumstances appropriate to the acceptance of such a belief, if he is disposed to make certain inferences on its basis, disposed to act in a way appropriate for one who has such a belief, prepared when circumstances warrant to impute such beliefs to other people, and so on. But to make such judgments about a person requires that we entertain many hypotheses about what he believes, desires, etc. and about how to construe other things he says: hence the reluctance to talk of meaning as something independent of general schemes for construing utterances and attributing beliefs, and the resistance to the idea that the perceptual beliefs which the phenomenalist takes to be epistemologically basic could stand alone. Phenomenalists have thought they could, the argument goes, because they have accepted the view that knowledge has two components, the brute fact element given to sense and the interpretative or conceptual element supplied by the mind, a view which encourages what Quine has called 'the myth of a museum in which the exhibits are meanings and the words are labels'.

But does a defender of phenomenalism have to hold that his basic beliefs could stand alone in the way that the parasitism argument implies? The obvious line of defence is to claim that phenomenalist theories are simply theories about relations of justification which hold between different kinds of beliefs. Such a view is reflected by Ayer's and Pollock's descriptivism and by Chisholm's view of epistemology as the logic of enquiry. Epistemology is said to be the analytic science of evidence. Someone who takes this line might say that a statement's expressing an epistemologically basic belief is compatible with there being a 'logical dimension' in which it is dependent on statements of a non-basic type, as in the case where a statement expressing a perceptual belief means what it does because of its fulfilling a certain role in a wider linguistic context. But to say that a belief is *epistemologically* basic is simply to claim that there is a certain asymmetry in the relations of justification which hold between it and other beliefs. There is no need to worry about whether it would be possible to have only epistemologically basic beliefs, or to have beliefs about how things look without having any beliefs about the physical world, and so the parasitism argument fails.

The argument of chapter three should make us somewhat suspicious of attempts to sever phenomenalist ideas from the doctrine of the given. We noted how the arguments intended to compel the recognition of epistemologically basic beliefs tended to trade on a view of epistemologically basic beliefs very like that presupposed by Rorty's parasitism argument. However, the best strategy at this point is to approach directly the question of whether any statement could express a belief which is 'epistemologically basic' or 'foundational' in a way that a phenomenalist theory of knowledge requires. The suspicion that phenomenalism is not easily detached from the doctrine of the given will be confirmed.

2. Intrinsic Credibility

We saw in chapter three that the foundational picture requires that basic beliefs be 'basic' in a very strong sense. The idea that knowledge rests on a foundation must be taken to preclude the possibility of there being even a potential regress of justification, otherwise the regress argument can be met by claiming that justification, for a given person or society, can come to an end with beliefs which are justifiable but for which the justification is not known.[15] Because the foundational view denies the possibility of there being even a potential regress of justification, a defender of this position will not be content with the admission that, since justification must come to an end somewhere, there must indeed be beliefs which are 'basic' in the sense of 'not thought to be open to challenge (in this context)'; or with the idea that non-inferential knowledge can be explicated in terms of there being beliefs the formation of which is empirically sufficient for their being true, or at least credible; or with the suggestion that the inferential/non-inferential distinction is simply the commonsense distinction between what we can report 'without thinking about it' (and are prepared to accept in the same way) and that which we reach only with intellectual effort (and/or that which seems intuitively to call for some justification). Rather the foundational view states that knowledge rests on a foundation of *absolutely* non-inferential knowledge: no further justification is either necessary or possible. As I put it, epistemologically basic beliefs must be intrinsically credible. The problem with this, however, is that no belief is worthy of credence *simply* in virtue of someone's holding it. Acceptability is always relative to further background knowledge. The traditional objection to this latter claim is that it involves us in a regress of justification, or commits us to a coherence theory of justification. In chapter three, I tried to show that such considerations do not compel the acceptance of a version of foundationalism.

The foundational view is the backbone of what I have been calling 'phenomenalism'. I have already argued that this approach to the theory of knowledge does not *have* to be correct. But when we reflect on the requirements which candidates for the foundational role have to meet, the question arises whether any theory along phenomenalist lines

[15] See above p. 71ff.

could be correct. How, that is, could there be beliefs which are epistemologically basic in the required sense?

Traditionally, it has been held that epistemologically basic beliefs are basic because incorrigible. However, we have so far left open the question of whether such beliefs need to be strictly incorrigible or whether they may be defeasible. Since the credibility of basic beliefs has to be intrinsic, the problem for one who wants to allow that they may be defeasible is to give an account of how their credibility can be intrinsic without being total. The usual way of achieving this end is to ground the credibility of basic beliefs in some conceptual or analytic truth. The idea is that it is analytically true that beliefs of that kind are true most of the time.[16] But this account of credibility is acceptable only if we are willing to countenance the notion of analytic truth. Of course, if we hold that it is just a matter of empirical fact that human perceivers are very good, though not infallible, when it comes to reporting on certain kinds of events, then it is easy to see how the beliefs they form about events of those kinds can be prima-facie justified but defeasible. But all such naturalistic accounts of the credibility attaching to observation statements, sensation reports and so on are inadmissible from a foundationalist point of view since they involve us in just the kind of regress of justification which foundationalism seeks to break out of by finding intrinsically credible—absolutely non-inferential—basic beliefs.

The idea that basic beliefs may be basic because incorrigible rests on a mistake. The question whether there are incorrigible beliefs is independent of whether there are such things as basic beliefs. The existence of basic beliefs cannot be established simply by arguing that beliefs of some particular kind—e.g. those expressed by first-person sensation reports—are incorrigible. It may be a tenet of our

[16] See, for example, Sidney Shoemaker, *Self-Knowledge and Self-Identity* (Ithaca: Cornell University Press, 1963).

commonsense view of the mind that a person's reports on his current mental states are incorrigible: that no evidence that you or I could adduce would be sufficient to override them. I do not know whether this is so (I am inclined to doubt it), but let us suppose for the sake of argument that it is. This supposition in no way supports the foundationalist view, since incorrigibility does not have to amount to absolutely non-inferential, or intrinsic, credibility. Reflecting our commonsense view of the mind, we have a linguistic practice of accepting a person's reports about his current mental states (more plausibly, his current thoughts and sensations) at face value. So long as we confine our attention to the individual report, no further justification is required or available, though we could cite reasons for our treating all reports *of that type* in the way that we do. And this is where a mistake can be made: the fact that, in the context of our ordinary attitude towards certain reports, no further justification is called for may tempt one into thinking that one has found a kind of belief which could constitute the rock-bottom foundation of empirical knowledge. Thus from the fact that in response to the question 'How do you know you are thinking about Albuquerque?' it would be natural to say 'I am, that's all', Chisholm concludes that such states are 'self-presenting' and that reports on such states express what is 'directly evident'—i.e. absolutely non-inferential.[17] But this is not so: the practice of accepting such reports at their face value is one component in a general theory—our commonsense view of the mind—which is empirically grounded and open to revision with the progress of enquiry. For the individual report, there is nothing that could be cited as its special justification, but there are reasons why we take all such reports to be credible in the way that we do. Not least of all, it is much easier to predict how people are going to react to various things if one takes seriously what they say

[17] Chisholm, op. cit., ch. 2.

about their thoughts and feelings. However, if a search for neurophysiological correlates of thought were carried to a successful conclusion, we might be led to revise any ideas we had about the ultimate epistemic authority of the individual in such matters.[18]

We have already rejected an appeal to the notion of truth in virtue of meaning as a way of explaining how epistemologically basic beliefs are possible: this follows from our having rejected analytic truth *tout court*. Now it turns out that a simple appeal to the special epistemic authority which a person might be thought to enjoy with respect to reports about his own thoughts and sensations is also inadequate. Even if the special authority amounts to incorrigibility, this is still something which a no-foundations view of knowledge can allow for. Of course, the kind of incorrigibility for which a no-foundations view can allow is not absolute incorrigibility, since it recognizes that the theory which gives certain reports this special status is open to modification. Rather the no-foundations view allows for relative incorrigibility, in much the same way as it allows for knowledge which is relatively a priori. The incorrigible status of reports about current thoughts and sensations (if indeed they have this status) is relative to a certain theory of the mind which might be revised or even given up entirely.[19] If a foundational theory of knowledge is to rest on the claim that basic beliefs are basic because incorrigible, the theory requires absolute incorrigibility, just as it requires (in

---

[18] We should, of course, have to begin by taking people's introspective reports at their face value. Some philosophers have thought that this would preclude our ever developing a theory which would enable us to override such reports. But just such a conceptual development has taken place with the adoption of the rapid-eye-movement criterion for dreaming.

[19] The position I take here presupposes that the traditional idea that certain inner states are simply given has been disposed of. The theoreticity of our notion of the mental is nicely illustrated by Sellars' story about our 'Rylean ancestors'. See his essay, 'Empiricism and the Philosophy of Mind', *Science, Perception and Reality*, ch. 5, sect. 45-63.

another context) knowledge which is absolutely a priori. But the existence of incorrigible beliefs in this highly technical sense cannot be established by pointing to our ordinary talk about such things as thoughts and sensations, any more than the existence of absolutely a priori principles of evidence can be established by pointing out that we have to have some views about what counts as evidence for what if any empirical investigation is to get off the ground.

The natural way to account for the credibility and non-inferential character of sensation reports, certain kinds of observation reports, and the like, is to look to the fact that human beings can be trained to respond directly to certain stimulus conditions and can thus reliably report on those conditions without pausing for thought. To the foundational theorist, it is obviously wrong-headed to try to account for the credibility attaching to a person's observation statements and so on by appealing to the reliability of human perceivers.[20] For the facts appealed to are general facts

That mentalistic discourse is something we might give up altogether is an immediate consequence of our rejecting the idea that we have a special prelinguistic awareness of our own mental states, an awareness to which any language has to be 'adequate'. That a materialist's desires might be as well satisfied by a withering away of mentalistic discourse as by our finding physical correlates for mental entities is a position which has come to be known as 'eliminative materialism'. The coherence of this position has been defended by W. V. Quine, 'Mental Entities', *Proceedings of the American Academy of Arts and Sciences*, LXXX (Boston, 1951), reprinted in John O'Connor, ed., *Modern Materialism* (New York: Harcourt, Brace and World, 1969), and by Richard Rorty, Mind-Body Identity, Privacy and Categories', *Review of Metaphysics*, XIX (1965), reprinted in O'Connor, op. cit. Eliminative materialism has been criticized by James Cornman, 'On the Elimination of 'Sensations' and Sensations', *Review of Metaphysics*, XXII (1968), also in O'Connor. Rorty has replied convincingly to Corman, 'In Defense of Eliminative Materialism', Review of Metaphysics, XXIV (1970).

[20] Accounts other than 'reliability' accounts of the special status of observation reports, perceptual beliefs, knowledge of one's own sensations, etc. have difficulties even in accounting for the simple fact that some of us are much more reliable as observers than others.

(worse still, from the standpoint of strict phenomenalists, they are stated in the physical-object language), and do not these need to be justified by particular observations? I considered various forms of this regress argument, genetic and non-genetic, in chapter three. What I want to call attention to now is how artificial are those phenomenalist accounts of observation statements which try to avoid appealing to empirical facts about human perceivers. The general idea has been that, if the credibility attaching to basic statements cannot be sought in the realm of empirical fact, it must somehow be established by an appeal to language: hence the attractiveness of the idea that it is a conceptual truth that in making certain first-person reports we are right most of the time. More popular has been the view that basic 'protocols', while not themselves analytically true, nevertheless resemble analytic statements in that their being correctly made is a sufficient as well as a necessary condition for their truth. This is harmless in itself and is compatible with a 'reliability' account of their credibility. The crunch comes when the notion of 'correctly making' is spelled out in terms of following the rules for words like 'red', where the rules in question are like those proposed by Ayer, rules which correlate 'symbols' with 'observable facts'. Since the facts are 'observable' without the aid of any 'symbols' we can see why philosophers who have taken this line have thought that, at the basic level, only verbal and not factual error is possible. Obviously, theories like this found empirical knowledge on the 'givenness' of basic phenomenal qualities. I have already commented at some length on the traditional doctrine of the given and shall not repeat those comments here.

Much of the debate over whether there could be such things as basic propositions has concerned the question of whether such propositions have to be 'comparative'. Opponents of basic propositions have argued that a proposition must either express a comparison or else be empty. But it is also claimed that expressing a comparison is incompatible with being epistemologically basic, and hence it is concluded that there is no such thing as a contentful basic proposition. I think that, in a number of ways, this discussion has been conducted in terms which tend to obscure rather than clarify the main points at issue.

A prominent figure in this debate is Reichenbach. In *Experience and Prediction,* he argues that statements reporting on sense-impressions, which many philosophers have taken to be epistemologically basic, give 'a comparison with a formerly seen object'.[21] One thing he has in mind is that we describe sense-impressions in terms of the kinds of object that normally give rise to such impressions. For example, we might describe a certain kind of flashing visual impression as being the kind of impression produced by a flash of lightning. If we apply this idea to colour-words, we will hold that, say, 'I am appeared to redly' means something like 'I am appeared to the way I am appeared to when I see something red under normal perceptual conditions.'

The problem is that, if this is the correct way to understand statements about appearances, then such statements will not express epistemologically basic beliefs. Knowing that one is appeared to in the way that one is appeared to when one sees something red under normal perceptual conditions presupposes all kinds of general knowledge—e.g. about how things which are objectively red normally appear, what kinds of conditions count as normal, and so on. As Chisholm puts it,

> . . . there would be no clear sense in which what is expressed by 'this appears white' could be said to be directly evident; to state our justification for thinking that we know that a certain thing appears white, we would need

---

[21] Hans Reichenbach, *Experience and Prediction* (Chicago: University of Chicago Press, Seventh Impression, 1970), p. 176.

to state our justification for our belief about the ways in which white things normally appear.[22]

Chisholm thinks that the way out is to distinguish between comparative and non-comparative uses of words. In its comparative use, 'I am appeared to redly' means 'I am appeared to in the way that red things normally appear to me.' Such a statement could not express an epistemologically basic belief or, as Chisholm would say, could not express what is directly evident. But there is another non-comparative use of terms like 'red' such that sentences like 'Red things normally appear red' make contingent statements. In this use, 'red' refers to a phenomenological state of the observer, and it is a contingent fact that red things normally produce this state rather than another.

There seems to be an implication here that there are two senses of 'red', the phenomenological sense and another, which we might call the 'physical' sense. It is worth noting that such a two-sense theory cannot readily be combined with the idea that basic beliefs constitute 'logical' reasons for higher-level beliefs. How can they if words like 'red' turn out to have two logically independent senses such that it is a contingent fact that red things normally look red? This is just where we are supposed to find analytic connexions.[23]

Pollock has suggested that Chisholm has a sound distinction in mind but fails to make clear what it is. The implied suggestion that words like 'red' may have two senses is particularly unfortunate. What we must distinguish are two ways of referring to a way of being appeared to.

[22] Chisholm, op. cit., pp. 35-36.
[23] This criticism applies to 'descriptivism' as defended by Ayer and Pollock. Chisholm has a more complicated theory of evidence designed to show how that which is only indirectly evident can be 'known through' that which is directly evident, although the relation between the directly and indirectly evident is neither inductive nor deductive. But it comes to much the same thing.

Referring 'comparatively' to a way of being appeared to involves referring to it as the way we are normally appeared in such and such circumstances. When we refer 'non-comparatively' to a way of being appeared to, we use a word or phrase which is 'associated directly with the phenomenological state'.[24]

This is a familiar move, and it faces a familiar difficulty. It seems that, in following this account of basic statements, we must fall into a dilemma. Thus Reichenbach:

> The objection may be raised that a comparison with formerly seen physical objects should be avoided, and that a basic statement is to concern the present fact only, as it is. But such a reduction would make the basic statement empty. Its content is just that there is a similarity between the present object and one formerly seen; it is by means of this relation that the present object is described. Otherwise the basic statement would consist in attaching an individual symbol, say a number, to the present object; but the introduction of such a symbol would help us in no way, since we could not make use of it to construct a comparison with other things.[25]

However, this argument is not altogether easy to follow. Clearly, a lot depends on what we understand by the claim that the judgments in question must be 'comparative' or assert 'a similarity between a present object and one formerly seen'.

An analysis of statements about appearances along the lines indicated by Reichenbach (and also by Bennett) suggests that statements about how one is appeared to are 'comparative' in a perfectly straightforward sense: such statements compare the way one is appeared to currently to

---

[24] Pollock, 'Perceptual Knowledge', op. cit., p. 313.
[25] Reichenbach, op. cit., p. 176.

the way one is appeared under certain standard perceptual conditions. One thing that a phenomenalist should object to here is that 'phenomenal' redness is explicated in terms of the objective redness of ordinary physical objects. But if a phenomenalist rejects the idea that judgments about how one is appeared to are 'comparative' in the sense of asserting that the way one is appeared to currently is like the way one would be appeared to in certain standard conditions, it is not at all obvious why he should be thought to be committed to the view that his 'phenomenal predicates' are non-comparative, in the sense of not being predicates at all, but rather names or 'individual symbols'.

Reichenbach does not always claim that a description of an impression commits one to comparing it to a previous impression of something that was in fact a physical object. Rather he says that it is sufficient that the previously experienced object was called, say, a flash of lightning. The content of a basic statement is that there is 'similarity between the present object and one formerly seen'; but what was formerly seen does not have to have been a physical object.[26]

It may be that he is entertaining a general view of predication to the effect that description always involves comparison. This would account for his claiming that basic statements are either comparative or else devoid of propositional content. But this view cannot be right, at least not if we understand 'comparative' in a commonsensical way. To say of a chair that it is like the one my friend bought last week is to make a judgment that is in the ordinary sense comparative, but to say that it is a chair is not. Descriptive content cannot always depend on comparison, in any ordinary sense: we can apply a description to an object even if it is the only object to which the description applies, or if it is the first object of that kind we have ever encountered. To

[26] Ibid., p. 176.

make plausible the argument that a statement must either be comparative or else lack propositional content, 'comparative' must be taken simply to mean 'descriptive', but this leaves it quite unclear why any phenomenalist should feel compelled to deny that his basic statements are comparative in *this* sense.

In spite of this, it is clear that many defenders of phenomenalism have taken very seriously the idea that a basic statement should, in a strong sense, concern 'the present fact only'. For example, Ayer argues that

> . . . if I use a sensory predicate to describe what I am now experiencing I need not make any claim about a situation other than the one before me. Accordingly, no appeal to such other situations can show that I am mistaken. They are not relevant since my statement makes no reference to them.[27]

As far as this argument goes, no use is made of the fact that 'sensory' predicates are under discussion. But suppose that I claim that there is a chair in the room that I am in now: there is no obvious sense in which I am making a claim about any situation other than the one before me. However, this does not mean that whatever claims I might make on other such occasions are completely irrelevant to whether my current claim is true or false, credible or not. On the contrary, facts about what I am inclined to say on other occasions are relevant to what I *mean* by my current claim. No statement I make, not even one involving a 'sensory' predicate, is ever as completely isolated from the rest of my dispositions to linguistic behaviour as Ayer seems to think.

By denying the relevance of all facts pertaining to 'other

[27] A. J. Ayer, 'Basic Propositions', in Max Black (ed.), *Philosophical Analysis* (Ithaca: Cornell University Press, 1950), reprinted in Ayer, *Philosophical Essays* (London: MacMillan, 1954). Page references to this edition. The passage quoted appears on p. 119.

situations', Ayer creates difficulties for his own position, for he is led to wonder whether claims involving his sensory predicates could have any propositional content at all. It seems that an act of naming is the only kind of linguistic act which could, with any plausibility, be held to be as self-contained as Ayer's claims involving sensory predicates are supposed to be.[28] Thus he feels that he is faced with a dilemma just like that posed by Reichenbach:

> Either I just name the situation, in which case I am not making any claim about it, and no question of truth or falsehood, knowledge or ignorance, certainty or uncertainty, arises; or else I describe it. And how can I describe it without relating it to something else?[29]

The anti-phenomenalist point behind the claim that all descriptive judgments make a comparison with a formerly perceived object is to call in question the idea that any such judgment, even one involving a sensory predicate, could be epistemologically basic. At the very least, in making such a comparative judgment, one is relying on knowledge of the past gained through memory. Ayer thus feels that he must rebut the charge that description always involves comparison. However, in so doing, he moves from the observation that statements involving sensory predicates can be non-comparative (in the sense that they do not make any explicit claims about 'other situations') to the conclusion that no facts about other situations are ever so much as relevant to the truth or credibility of these statements. This is a fallacy, and the dilemma which Ayer finds himself facing is a false one. A statement does not have to be either explicitly comparative or else so completely self-contained that no facts about other situations are even relevant to its truth or

[28] And whatever plausibility lies here derives from a commitment to the doctrine of the given.

[29] Ayer, op. cit., p. 119.

credibility. Thus in order to rebut the charge that a statement involving a sensory predicate has to be comparative, it is not necessary to defend the idea that basic statements must somehow be absolutely non-comparative: non-comparative in a sense which threatens the possibility of their having any descriptive content at all.

However, although it is possible for a phenomenalist like Ayer to escape this particular dilemma, the fact that no statement is ever so completely self-contained that facts about other situations are quite irrelevant to its truth or to its credibility suggests another line of attack on the notion of a basic statement. Chisholm states the argument as follows:

> (a) In saying 'Something appears white', you are making certain assumptions about language; you are assuming, for example, that the word 'white', or the phrase 'appears white', is being used in the way in which other people have used it. Therefore (b), when you say 'This appears white', you are saying something not only about your present experience, but also about all of these other occasions. But (c) what you are saying about these other occasions is not directly evident. And therefore (d), 'This is white' does not express what is directly evident.[30]

Chisholm does not think that this argument need trouble the proponent of basic statements. The false step, he says, lies in the inference from (a) to (b):

> We must distinguish the belief that a speaker has about the words that he is using from the belief that he is using these words to express . . .
> . . . it may be that what a man believes about his own use of the expression 'appears white' is something that is not directly evident to him—indeed what he believes about his

[30] Chisholm, op. cit., pp. 36-37.

own language may be false and unreasonable; but from
these facts it does not follow that what he intends to assert
when he utters 'This appears white to me' is something
that cannot be directly evident.[31]

This is true. It does not follow from the fact that in making a
particular statement one may also be making certain
'assumptions about language' that one is giving voice to
those assumptions when one makes the statement. However,
the critic of basic statements need make no such claim. It is
sufficient for his purposes that these background
assumptions be relevant to the statement's truth or
credibility: in order to be relevant, they do not have to be
stated. And surely such assumptions are relevant.
Furthermore, they are not simply 'assumptions about
language' in any special sense: they are just as much
assumptions about the perceptual capabilities of the person
making the statement. Knowing the meaning of an
observational term like 'white' is not to be divorced from
having the ability to report reliably on the presence of white
things. But as we saw earlier, reference to empirical facts
about the reliability of perceivers is just what the
foundationalist wants to avoid in his account of the
credibility of basic observation statements. So although
Chisholm is right to complain that the inference from (a) to
(b) is invalid, his criticism does not really detract from the
force of the argument since premise (a) alone promises to
give the opponent of basic statements all he needs.
    If this argument is correct, the intuition which has led
phenomenalists to rely heavily on ostension in their accounts
of basic statements is not to be lightly dismissed. A further
reason for adopting a theory along these lines might be a
desire to guarantee the absolute incorrigibility of basic
statements by safeguarding them from the possibility of even

[31] Ibid., p. 37.

verbal error. Thus Pollock argues that basic beliefs are expressed by sentences like 'I am appeared to *that* way', where the reference of 'that' is secured by 'a kind of mental pointing, a focussing of attention'.[32] The reference 'cannot be secured by a description or an expression whose denotation is fixed by its conventional meaning'.[33] This demonstrative reference ensures incorrigibility. 'That' refers to the way I am appeared to, so my belief that I am appeared to *that* way is true just in case I am appeared to that way. We noted earlier that de facto incorrigibility is insufficient for a foundational theory of knowledge and that defenders of such theories have tried to make the credibility of basic statements a matter of language rather than a matter of fact. Pollock's theory is in this tradition: he is arguing that, although basic statements are not analytic, nevertheless the form of words used guarantees the truth of what is said.

How could any theory like this ever hope to work? In particular, how could such mental pointing secure reference? Pollock gives an example: encountering an old oak tree I remember only dimly, I mutter 'So *that* is the way the tree is shaped'. Or suppose that the tree is a familiar one, but I have been taking hallucinogenic drugs. In this case I may look at the tree and think to myself 'But *that* is not the way the tree is shaped.' In the second case, 'that' refers to a shape, but not to the shape of the tree. Rather, in both cases, we should say that 'that' refers to a shape to which I am attending.[34]

Does this example help? It seems to me that, even here, the demonstrative is able to function, if at all, only within a descriptive context. That is to say, I must at least be able to represent to myself that it is the shape and not e.g. the colour that I intend to pick out. But the whole point of theories like the one we are considering is to insist that the demonstrative can be used to refer without any descriptive mediation. Such

[32] Pollock *Perceptual Knowledge*, p. 315.
[33] Ibid., p. 315.
[34] Ibid., p. 316.

theories cannot in the end be understood apart from the traditional idea that basic phenomenal qualities are simply 'given'. Only if it is claimed that we have pre-linguistic awareness of these basic qualities is it plausible to hold that we can refer to them without any descriptive mediation simply by a kind of 'mental pointing' or focussing of attention. Again, when we try to think phenomenalist theories through, we find the doctrine of the given lurking in the background. Pollock's notion of 'pure mental pointing' is strangely reminiscent of the 'pure inspection' which Price proposed as the method by which the perceptual foundations of knowledge, the sense-data given to the mind, were to be studied, which illustrates nicely how little the basic ideas behind phenomenalistic theories have changed.

Even if we were to grant that mental pointing of the requisite degree of purity were possible, any attempt to salvage a foundationalist theory of knowledge by appealing to the notion of pure ostension would still face insuperable difficulties. To begin with, it is hard to see how such an account of basic statements could be combined with the idea that basic statements constitute logical reasons, or criteria, for statements about the physical world. Proponents of criteria argue that meaning is determined, at least in part, by justification conditions. Thus it is said that 'I am appeared to redly' is a logical reason for me to believe that there is something red before me, in virtue of the meaning of 'red'. But if the being-appeared-to-redly aspect of my perceptual experience is picked out by pure mental pointing, the concept of redness will not be exercised in the basic belief and the argument for the meaning-link between basic and non-basic beliefs will no longer apply.

For many defenders of phenomenalistic theories, this would be bad enough; but there is a much more serious and more general objection. That is that beliefs expressed by statements like 'I am appeared to *that* way' are far too weak to serve as a foundation for our knowledge of the physical world. No version of phenomenalism holds that any sense-history whatever could justifiably be described as experience of an objective world. Phenomenalism bases our knowledge of the world on the ability to recognize and project a certain pattern or order within experience. But if the beliefs which express presentational content turn out to be expressed by statements of the form of 'I am appeared to *that* way', where the reference of 'that' is secured by pure mental pointing, it is hard to see how progress could be made. For we would have only '*That* way' and at a later time '*That* way', whereas to recognize patterns or to make inductively based projections we need not just '*That* way' but 'The *same* way as before'. To recognize similarities, we have to make descriptive judgments, and describing does not bring with it a logical guarantee of success. When we apply it to a theory like the one presented by Pollock, Reichenbach's objection that it would be useless to attach an individual symbol to an experience since the mere attaching of such a symbol would not permit us to 'construct a comparison' is perfectly sound.[35]

I remarked earlier that one reason behind the appeal to ostension could be a desire to make epistemologically basic statements safe from the possibility of even 'verbal' error. As Pollock puts it, it is always possible when expressing a basic belief for a person to 'use the wrong words to refer to the phenomenological state he has in mind'.[36] It is worth noting an ambiguity in the notion of having a phenomenological state in mind. On the one hand, this might come to no more than simply being in the state, in which case there is no reason to suppose that the person is entertaining any particular belief about the way he is appeared to: he is

[35] These considerations about the use of 'same' lie at the heart of Wittgenstein's attack in his *Philosophical Investigations* on the idea of private ostensive definition.

[36] Pollock, op. cit., p. 313.

simply being appeared to in some way or other. However, if anyone were to think of this state, not in itself a cognitive state at all, as nevertheless being a kind of belief, he might be seduced by the fact that there is nothing to be wrong about here into thinking that he had isolated a specially privileged kind of belief, missing the fact that, although there is nothing to be wrong about, there is nothing to be right about either. This is the kind of error we find in the writings of C. I. Lewis who wrote that the import of the claim that knowledge has a given basis is 'simply that there is such a thing as experience'.[37] The other sense of 'having in mind' is 'thinking about'. This involves more than just being in a phenomenological state: there must also be some way of representing the contents of the state in thought. The idea I have been trying to undermine is that the beliefs we form about our phenomenological states are intrinsically credible and hence suitable to serve as a foundation for empirical knowledge.

We have seen that grave difficulties confront attempts to formulate statements expressing epistemologically basic beliefs, and we have been led to wonder whether any beliefs could be 'basic' in the sense required by phenomenalistic theories of knowledge. This might encourage us to take Lewis's remark a bit more seriously. Perhaps a defender of phenomenalism can find his way out of these problems by claiming that justification terminates ultimately, not with beliefs about experiences, but with states of some other kind—the experiences themselves, say. I think that Bennett may incline towards this view, and this might explain why he does not consider the problems which we found to arise out of his attempt to combine phenomenalism with his 'anti-reificationist' analysis of sense-data. Let us recall his two analyses of the sentence 'He has a Ø sense-datum':

[37] C. I. Lewis, *An Analysis of Knowledge and Valuation*, p. 182.

(1)   It is with him as though he were perceiving a . . .

(2)   He is sensorily affected in the way he usually is when
       he perceived a . . .[38]

My thought was that, taken as they stand, neither of these
implies that the perceiver is in any kind of cognitive state,
that he is entertaining a perceptual judgment as opposed to
merely being sensorily affected. Thus merely having sense-
data cannot constitute the basic mode of empirical
knowledge. This must involve *knowing that* one is having
such-and-such a sense-datum. This is what I took Bennett's
position to be, and he does claim that 'one's evidence for
what is objectively the case consists in or rests ultimately
upon facts about one's own sensory states', taking sense-
data in the spirit of the anti-reification thesis. This is what
leads to the problems I discussed above. But Bennett
sometimes seems to hold that justification terminates
ultimately not with knowing facts about one's sensory states,
but simply with the states themselves, as e.g. in his
preparedness to equate being in sensory states with
confronting 'raw chunks of reality'.[39] His explication of the
notion of a sense-datum seemed to create problems because it
seemed that, in order to know any statements about sense-
data to be true, one would need already to know a good deal
about the objective world of persons and physical things.
However, if his view is that the bedrock of empirical
knowledge consists simply of being in sensory states, no such
problems arise.

We can see, then, why the view that the foundation of
empirical knowledge consists in the experiences themselves
might be attractive. However, the view dismisses the
problems connected with basic statements and beliefs only at

[38] Bennett, op. cit., p. 33.
[39] Ibid., p. 136.

the cost of making unintelligible the notion of a perceptual foundation for knowledge. For if the having of an experience is not a state the content of which is expressible in a perceptual judgment, then there is no way for 'experiences' to serve as a check on anything, to count in favour of one hypothesis rather than another. Our criticism of this theory follows closely our criticism in chapter two of the idea that empirical knowledge rests on our being 'given' sense-data, or is in some other way 'non-propositional': in both cases we are left completely in the dark as to how the alleged foundation of knowledge is supposed to perform the task demanded of it.

In sum, I do not think that the theory that knowledge rests simply on 'experiences' or the theory that it rests on our knowing ways of being appeared to simply as '*That way*' are significantly different. In both cases, we have more or less found our way back to Bradley's conception of immediate experience as something which is nothing for the intellect, the content of which is knowable only as 'this'. I remarked that, if immediate experience is knowable only as 'this', Bradley's insistence that all our knowledge of the world 'must submit to pass through it' cannot but strike us as futile. I have seen no reason to change that verdict.

3. CONCLUSION

I think, then, that the idea that empirical knowledge rests on any kind of a foundation is something that we should give up entirely. This is not to say that the quest for a foundation for knowledge was without point. On the contrary, the point behind attempts to place knowledge on a foundation was to show how genuine knowledge might be distinguished from idle fancy or blind prejudice, to show why empirical knowledge, properly so-called, is far from being, in Lewis's phrase, 'contentless and arbitrary'. In the end, the motivation was a moral one. But by its own standards, the theory is a failure, and on two counts. First of all, an acceptance of the foundational view leaves us with no adequate defence against the sceptical argument. Once we accept the idea of a strict epistemological order, we cannot explain how a warranted inference to the existence of the physical world is possible. And secondly, no convincing account can be given of how there could be such things as intrinsically credible basic beliefs even though, according to the foundational view, without such beliefs nothing else can be justified.

Once we abandon the foundational view, our knowledge of the physical world is secure. There is a sense in which the no-foundations view amounts to a defence of direct realism: for I should certainly want to hold that non-inferential knowledge of acts about physical objects is possible, though this knowledge is not non-inferential in the sense required by phenomenalistic theories of knowledge.[40] Once our knowledge of the commonsense physical world is secure, then Ayer's scientific approach—which amounts to nothing more than the truism that, by confining its attention exclusively to induction by simple enumeration, the sceptical argument, as originally formulated, takes altogether too narrow a view of empirical inference—is adequate to rescue us from the threat of special applications of the sceptical argument against our claims to have knowledge of entities belonging to a higher level of theoreticity. So there is a sense in which, in the long run, I want to look favourably on 'the scientific approach'. My objection was to the Humean theory, according to which our knowledge of physical objects can be seen as the result of a theoretical inference from the 'coherence' of experience. But this is not to say that I am advocating a strict epistemological order, restricted in my case to knowledge of commonsense physical objects

[40] See above, ch. 3, sect. 3.

versus knowledge of theoretical entities; for I do not wish to set any a priori limits to the kinds of things on which, with suitable training, we might come to report directly. It is an empirical matter entirely. There is no a priori reason why we should not come to report directly on things which, by other criteria, might be thought to belong to a higher level of theoreticity: our own mental states are a case in point.

Nowhere in my argument have I attempted to offer strict analyses of such concepts as 'observational knowledge'. Rather, at various points, I have tried to suggest an alternative picture of knowledge and justification to that offered by the foundational view and its comrade-in-arms, the doctrine of the given. Instead of the picture of knowledge as an edifice resting on fixed and immutable foundations, I want to offer the picture of human knowledge as an evolving social phenomenon. At any time, we will have a solid core of unquestioned perceptual reports, and the like, against which more marginal and less certain beliefs can be checked. But even this solid core may come in for drastic revision in the interests of deeper insight or theoretical advance. Any belief can be questioned, though not all at once. In this way, the pursuit of empirical knowledge can be seen as a rational pursuit not because empirical knowledge rests on a foundation but because, as Sellars puts it, it is a self-correcting enterprise.

In some ways, I think that to suggest an alternative picture is the most important task, since I think that it is perhaps the only way in which the grip of the foundational view on the philosophical imagination can be broken: we need a new gestalt, a shift of perspective. Genuine arguments for the foundational view are not easy to find, but it cannot be denied that the picture of knowledge it presents is capable of taking a powerful hold. Accepting the foundational view is, as Wittgenstein would say, like letting a particular metaphor or picture occupy a very central place in one's way of looking at things. Ultimately, it is not a viable way but, for all that, it is attractive at a very deep level. I suspect that to account for the power of its appeal, or to locate its source, we should have to look beyond the realms of philosophical argument as it is usually understood.

Much of the history of philosophy since Descartes has been the history of epistemology. I suggested in chapter one that the concern of epistemology has been to place human knowledge on its proper foundation. If we can break the grip of the foundational view on our philosophical imagination, we shall have reached the stage, envisioned by Wittgenstein, where we can stop doing that kind of philosophy when we want to.

Afterword

1. Introductory Remarks

Four topics stand in particular need of elaboration: the idea of epistemic justification, the foundational picture of knowledge and justification, the sense in which rejection of that picture leads to a "coherentist" epistemology, and whether abandoning the project of identifying foundations for knowledge is tantamount to the death of epistemology.

2. Aspects of Justification

The main reason for thinking that there must be epistemologically basic beliefs is that such beliefs are necessary to block a vicious infinite regress of reasons for reasons for reasons, and so on without end. Accordingly, the heart of *Groundless Belief* is the discussion in Chapter three of this argument.

Today, I prefer to think of the regress argument as "the Agrippan Problem," after Agrippa, the ancient sceptic who seems first to have given it clear articulation. The problem revolves around a destructive yet apparently inescapable trilemma. According to the Agrippan sceptic, any attempt to justify a claim either opens a vicious regress or terminates in one of two unsatisfactory ways: we run out of things to say, thus making an ungrounded assumption; or we find ourselves repeating some claim or claims already entered, thus reasoning in a circle. Thinking of this argument as "the regress problem" puts us in danger of underestimating its force. Stressing the need to cut off the regress may lead us to suppose that one of the other options *must* be defensible. However, the Agrippan problem is to avoid the regress without lapsing into circularity or brute assumption.[1] Stating the problem in terms of the trilemma helps us remember this.

A natural initial reaction to the Agrippan problem is that there is something artificial about it. To be sure, there are situations in which disputes run into an Agrippan dead end, but this is hardly the rule. Satisfactory justifications for disputed claims can be given by finding evidence that is acceptable to all parties. This is what is ordinarily called "justification."

The Agrippan sceptic will not deny this. What he will say is that "evidence acceptable to all parties" is simply evidence *accepted* by all parties, i.e., assumptions that all parties are willing to make. However, where this kind of justification is entirely *dialectical*, epistemic justification is supposed to be objectively truth-conducive. Justification that rests on mere assumptions— no matter how widely shared—does not meet this standard.

I argue in Chapter three that the need to cut off the regress does not force us to accept the foundationalist doctrine of intrinsic credibility: there are various ways in which justified beliefs can be "noninferential." I conclude that we should resist the temptation to offer any account of "the essential nature of justification." However, not knowing when to stop, I add:

> If I had to offer an aphoristic statement of the essential nature of justification, I should probably say that being justified consists in doing or saying what your conscience and your society let you get away with. This is a vacuous remark, but it is meant to be. (p. 115)

Of course, this remark is not vacuous at all. Indeed, it appears to concede the Agrippan sceptic's point that, if there are no foundations for knowledge, justification becomes purely dialectical.

---

[1] See Robert Fogelin, *Pyrrhonian Reflections on Knowledge and Justification* (Oxford and New York: Oxford University Press 1994), ch. 6. However, Fogelin is less sanguine than I am about our prospects for responding to the Agrippan argument. For a critical response to Fogelin's claim to have defended scepticism, see my "Fogelin's Neo-Pyrrhonism," *International Journal of Philosophical Studies* (1999).

In fact, I do not ignore the demand for an objective dimension to justification. On the contrary, I express some sympathy for the idea that, in some cases at least, justification may properly be understood in an "externalist" or "reliabilist" way. However, to issue this reminder is to invite the objection that my position is simply inconsistent.

I gesture towards a reliabilist view of knowledge in Chapter three, where I offer two strategies for responding to the regress argument in its "genetic" form. Thus:

> If we agree that knowing always requires being able to jus-tify, we will follow Sellars and deny that our present knowl-edge of certain general facts like "X is a reliable symptom of Y" depends on our having had prior knowledge of the relevant particular facts. We will say that our ability to give reasons now is built on a long history of language-learning, certain episodes in which—e.g., utterances of "This is green"—were no doubt "superficially like those which are later properly said to express observational knowledge." But the likeness is superficial. In the absence of the ability to justify, it would be incorrect to describe such episodes as expressions of observa-tional knowledge. On the other hand, if we do not insist quite so rigorously on the ability to justify, we can allow these ear-lier episodes . . . to count as expressions of knowledge, with-out thereby committing ourselves to a foundationalist account of their credibility. . . . I do not choose between the two ap-proaches because I have no clear intuitions about how much justifying a person has to be able to do before he counts as knowing. (pp. 95–6)

This passage may suggest that I would be open to blocking the regress with the aid of a purely reliabilist—what would now be thought of as a purely externalist—account of observational knowledge. However, I did not think then and do not think now that knowledge and justification can be decisively separated in the way that radical externalists suppose. At the same time, I do not think that justification should be understood in a purely dialectical fashion either.

It is unfortunate that I present the externalist option as part of
a criticism of Sellars, since I do not in any way intend to repudiate Sellars's core idea that "In characterizing an episode or state
as that of *knowing*, we are not giving an empirical description of
that episode or state; we are placing it in the logical space of
reasons, of justifying and being able to justify what one says."[2]
Accordingly, my endorsement of the externalist option is importantly qualified. I say that "we might count a child's early observation reports as expressing knowledge because they are *in fact*
reliable (and are justifiable by a fully-fledged language-user,
thus making the child a *potential* justifier) even though the child
could not be expected to marshal facts about his linguistic capabilities in support of his observational claims" (p. 94). What I
should have stressed is the point that *we* can ascribe knowledge
to subjects who are in no position to ascribe it to themselves.
The beliefs and claims of participants (and perhaps fledgling
participants) in what Sellars calls "the game of giving and asking for reasons" can inherit positive epistemic status from the
beliefs and claims of other participants with whom they interact.
Knowledge is always connected with justification, but one need
not always be in a position to provide all the information relevant to justifying one's beliefs. The thought that the theory of
knowledge must concern itself first and foremost with the sort of
justification available to the "individual knowing subject" is another aspect of the foundationalist picture I am trying to call into
question.

There is, then, no incompatibility between my willingness to
recognise an element of truth in externalist reliabilism and my
apparent commitment to a fundamentally dialectical conception
of justification. However, my discussion of these matters would

[2] "Empiricism and the Philosophy of Mind," p. 169. This essay has now
been re-issued as a stand-alone piece: Wilfrid Sellars, *Empiricism and the Philosophy of Mind*, with an Introduction by Richard Rorty and study guide by
Robert Brandom (Cambridge MA: Harvard University Press 1997). Quotation
p. 76 in this new edition.

have been significantly clearer if I had distinguished two aspects of justification. These are, to use Robert Fogelin's useful terminology, epistemic responsibility and adequate grounding.[3] A *person* is *justified in believing* a given proposition—let us say personally justified—when he or she forms or holds that belief in an epistemically responsible way. A person's *belief* is justified if there are grounds that make the proposition believed likely to be true.

Together with Hilary Kornblith, Fogelin holds that knowledge requires both sorts of justification. I think that Kornblith and Fogelin are right about this. One of the main arguments against pure externalism is that we are very reluctant to ascribe knowledge to someone who has formed a belief by a method that he has good reason to think unreliable, even if he is wrong about his method's unreliability. Although he meets the externalist criterion of *de facto* reliability, such a person is epistemically irresponsible and so fails to have knowledge. But we are equally reluctant to ascribe knowledge to someone who has formed a belief by an unreliable method, even if his circumstances render his use of the method epistemically blameless. Reliability without responsibility and responsibility without reliability: both disqualify us from knowing.

Accepting the distinction between epistemic responsibility and adequate grounding does not commit us to any particular account of what either consists in. In some cases, epistemic responsibility may require the ability to cite evidence for what one believes. But there may be cases in which one is responsible provided one has not been seriously negligent, for example by ignoring counter-evidence that one ought to have taken into account. A similar point can be made about grounding. An adequately grounded belief may be one that is inferred from appropriate evidence. But, for all that has been said, a belief may also be adequately grounded when unself-consciously formed by a reliable method. How epistemic responsibility and grounding re-

[3] Hilary Kornblith, "Ever Since Descartes," *The Monist* (1985), pp. 264–276. Fogelin, *Pyrrhonian Reflections,* ch. 1.

late to each other, and how each should be understood, are both matters for further argument.[4]

We gain real insight into foundationalism by seeing it as taking a particular view of the relation between epistemic responsibility and grounding, a view that has definite implications for how both aspects of justification are to be understood. For the foundationalist, justified belief is subject to what I now call the Prior Grounding Requirement: the insistence that epistemically responsible believing is always and everywhere believing on the basis of citable evidence. We may be "practically" or "pragmatically" justified in holding beliefs without such evidence, but this is not *epistemic* justification.

This conception of justification excludes all sorts of otherwise attractive possibilities: that evidential justification can be socially distributed; that grounding may sometimes be understood along externalist lines; and that there may be epistemic entitlement without evidence of any kind. In fact, the Prior Grounding Requirement leads straight to the demand for epistemologically basic beliefs. Since we cannot make good on this demand, we should drop the conception of justification that enforces it.

On the "Prior Grounding" conception of justification, little turns on the distinction between personal justification and grounding: obviously so, since the Prior Grounding Requirement makes grounding-by-evidence the only route to epistemic responsibility. The distinction comes into its own only when we drop the Requirement, for then the possibility opens up that the relation between epistemic responsibility and the possession of evidence is much more complicated than the foundationalist picture allows. This brings me to Sellars's tantalising but undeveloped idea that empirical knowledge is rational, not because it rests on foundations, but because it is a self-correcting enterprise.

I suggest that we take Sellars to be recommending that we see justified belief as conforming to what Robert Brandom calls a

---

[4] Fogelin, *Pyrrhonian Reflections*, p. 46f.

"default and challenge structure."[5] For a competent adult, across a wide range of situations, justification is a default condition: such a person is deemed epistemically responsible and his beliefs adequately grounded unless there is reason to suspect otherwise. One can be justified without having *gone through* a process of justification. Actively justifying—marshaling evidence and so on—is required only in the face of a reasonable challenge to one's epistemic responsibility or to the adequacy of one's grounds (which, remember, need not be *evidence*). Naturally, since there is not usually much point in stating the obvious, claims worth making often face standing objections or provoke immediate challenges. Such claims, therefore, will often not enjoy default justification but rather require defence; if they cannot be adequately defended, they must be modified or withdrawn. This is how knowledge grows by self-correction.

Notice, in this connection, the importance of justification as grounding. In laying claim to knowledge, though we do not always need to *demonstrate* adequate grounding, we are *committed* to it. This commitment is an important source of challenges. If reasons can be adduced for supposing that a belief of mine was formed in some unreliable way, I can maintain epistemic responsibility only by allaying this suspicion. It is vital to our dialectical practice of giving and asking for reasons that we do not understand justification in purely dialectical terms. Epistemically impeccable behaviour does not guarantee knowledge.

This brings me back to my ill-considered remark identifying justification with social permission. Recognising the social dimension of justification, dimly perceiving justification's default and challenge structure, but failing to draw clearly the distinction between epistemic responsibility and groundedness, I find myself tempted by a purely dialectical conception of justification as *simply* the capacity to meet whatever objections one's epistemic community throws out. While this is a reasonable account of personal justification, it ignores the way that challenges

[5] Robert Brandom, *Making It Explicit* (Cambridge MA: Harvard University Press 1994), ch. 4.

to personal justification arise out of suspicions concerning the objective adequacy of one's grounds. Instead of suggesting a partially externalist idea of "grounding" as an alternative response to the regress problem, I should have argued that a non-foundationalist theory of knowledge gains plausibility by combining dialectical and reliabilist elements.

3. FOUNDATIONS VERSUS COHERENCE

Rejecting the foundational conception of knowledge and justification, I opt for what I present as a "trivial" form of coherentism. The view is supposed to be trivial because "coherentist" only in the sense of "non-foundational." Today, I would describe the view I was reaching for as "contextualist" rather than "coherentist." I think that contextualism and coherentism offer very different conceptions of "knowledge without foundations."

Coherence theories are sometimes characterised by their commitment to the idea that "only a belief can justify a belief." This idea is indeed trivial if all it means is that only things that we are aware of can be *cited in justification* of a disputed claim. But if it means that only things we are aware of are relevant to the epistemic standing of our claims or beliefs, it is not trivial but false, for the reasons just given.

In any case, I do not think that the idea that justification is entirely a matter of belief-belief relations is sufficient to capture the coherentist outlook. Coherence theories properly so-called are *radically holistic*. A given belief inherits its positive epistemic status by virtue of being a member of a coherent "total view." Justification depends on properties of belief systems *considered as wholes*. For a contextualist, by contrast, justification depends on our holding beliefs or entering claims that are epistemically acceptable in a particular context of inquiry. Contextualism finds no use for the coherentist's idea of "global" justification.

Distinguishing between contextualism and the coherence theory commits me to clarifying my idea of a foundational approach to knowledge. It becomes important to distinguish two forms of foundationalism, formal and substantive.

> *Formal Foundationalism.* Justification requires beliefs that are *in some sense* justifiably held without resting on further evidence.
>
> *Substantive Foundationalism.* There are certain kinds of beliefs that, by their very nature, play the role of terminating points for chains of justification. These beliefs are epistemologically basic because *intrinsically credible* or *self-evidencing.*

Central to substantive foundationalism is the doctrine that I now call "epistemological realism": the idea that there are broad kinds of beliefs standing in fixed relations of epistemic priority. Substantive foundationalism is committed to there being natural epistemic kinds, ordered by natural epistemic relations.[6] Substantive foundationalism is foundationalism proper. It is my target in *Groundless Belief.*

Because contextualism recognises default justification, it is formally foundationalist. However, whether a belief enjoys default status will depend on a large number of contextually variable factors: for example, the particular inquiry in which we are engaged and what objections, if any, are currently in play. Not only is default justification not an intrinsic characteristic of any particular kind of belief: abstracting from all contextual considerations, no belief or claim has any particular epistemic standing. Contextualism is the antithesis of substantive foundationalism.

Substantive foundationalism is atomistic. Intrinsic credibility attaches to each basic belief, irrespective of what other beliefs a person may hold, the context of inquiry to which the belief is relevant, or the believer's real-world situation. The same goes

---

[6] For a detailed development of this idea see my *Unnatural Doubts: Epistemological Realism and the Basis of Scepticism* (Oxford: Blackwell 1992; paperback edition, Princeton N.J.: Princeton University Press 1996). For a systematic development of a contextualist epistemology, see my *Problems of Knowledge* (Oxford: Oxford University Press 1999).

for the epistemic relations between basic and non-basic beliefs. This is why, in explaining the relationship of basic to non-basic beliefs, foundationalism gravitates towards an appeal to meaning. However, while contextualism repudiates substantive foundationalism's epistemological atomism, it does not embrace radical holism. According to contextualism, justification always presupposes a *critical epistemic mass* of contextually relevant beliefs. No belief, considered alone, is ever justified or justifies any other belief. But this does not imply any theoretical use for the idea of a "total view."

From a contextualist standpoint, both foundationalism and the coherence theory are over-reactions to the Agrippan problem. Accepting that fixed points are required to cut off the regress of justification, the substantive foundationalist postulates a stratum of intrinsically credible basic beliefs. Against the foundationalist, the coherence theorist argues that individual beliefs always owe their justificational status and significance to relations with further beliefs, so that the demand for intrinsic credibility cannot be met. However, he moves straight from this repudiation of epistemological atomism to radical holism, with its own characteristic problems. By allowing for both fixed points and epistemic inter-dependence, contextualism offers a way between the horns of this dilemma.

4. The Tribunal of Experience

With these various clarifications in hand, I can locate the argument of *Groundless Belief* with respect to recent important work by John McDowell.[7] Some of McDowell's key moves are very similar to moves I make in *Groundless Belief*. McDowell rejects the idea of the Given for reasons very like those I rehearse in Chapter two. He also finds incoherent attempts to view empiri-

---

[7] John McDowell, *Mind and World*, paperback edition (Cambridge MA: Harvard University Press, 1996). For further discussion of McDowell's diagnosis of the ills of modern philosophy, see my review-article "Exorcism and Enchantment," *Philosophical Quarterly* (1996).

cal knowledge "from sideways on": that is, with our system of beliefs "circumscribed within a boundary, and the world outside it."[8] I concur. As I say in the main text:

> One can become haunted by the picture of one's belief system incorporating all sorts of internal relations of justification while, as a whole, floating above the world with no point of contact. But this worry is incoherent, because the concept of "the world" which is operative here is completely vacuous. (p. 101)

To this extent, McDowell is right to insist on what he calls "the unboundedness of the conceptual." There is no worthwhile question to be asked about the relation of "our beliefs" to the world as an unspecifiable thing-in-itself.

These significant areas of agreement notwithstanding, McDowell ends up with a view of empirical knowledge very different from mine. McDowell sees modern philosophy as caught on the horns of a dilemma, oscillating between the Myth of the Given and what he calls "frictionless" coherentism. I have no doubt that he would regard *Groundless Belief* as one more illustration of this oscillation.

McDowell's aim is to make sense of a "minimal empiricism." The mind-world relation involved in judgment or belief is "normative" in the sense that "thinking that aims at judgment, or at the fixation of belief, is answerable to the world—to how things are—for whether or not it is correctly executed." So far as knowledge of the empirical world is concerned, this means that judgment and belief are answerable to "how things are in so far as how things are is empirically accessible." Our judgments and beliefs must be subject to verdicts from the "tribunal of experience."[9] But it can be difficult to understand how it is possible for experience to constitute a tribunal to which judgment is accountable.

---

[8] McDowell, *Mind and World*, p. 34.

[9] Ibid., p. xii. The Introduction to the paperback edition of *Mind and World* sheds much light on McDowell's philosophical motives.

What we want to understand is how, through experience, our judgments and beliefs can be subject to *rational* control by *the world*. The appeal to the Given is on the right lines, in that the given element in experience, as non-conceptual, is external to thought. However, precisely because it is non-conceptual, the Given is incapable of providing a rational check on judgment or belief. Whatever validates or invalidates our judgments must be capable of standing in logical relations to them, and nothing lacking propositional content can enter into such relations. At best, the Given can exert a causal influence on our judgments and beliefs. But, although causes can sometimes exculpate, they can never justify.

Recognising the Given as a myth seems to force us to adopt some form of coherentism. However, because the only justificational relations coherentism recognises are those between judgments or beliefs and further judgments or beliefs, coherentism loses the element of control by the world altogether, becoming "frictionless." We seem forced to choose between external control that is not rational and rational control that is not external. Since neither option is satisfactory, we oscillate between them.

McDowell's solution is to urge us to see experience itself as conceptual through and through. He takes this to imply that, in experience, we see that things are thus and so: we simply take in how things are; we are open to the world. Of course, we can get things wrong: our openness to the world is fallible. However, we should not conclude from our fallibility that we never simply see how things are, even when we get things right. In McDowell's view, there is no compulsory move from the fact of fallibility to what he calls the "highest common factor" view of experience, the view that, since we do not always experience the world as it really is, the content of experience must have to do with appearances.

McDowell's conception of experience as taking in "manifest facts" requires that the world itself contain "thinkable contents." Such contents belong to "the layout of reality." McDowell argues that this possibility seems foreclosed by our modern naturalistic conception of the world as a realm of law. This disenchanted conception of the world, which admits only objects standing in nomological relations, makes no room in the world for such things as thinkable contents. The solution is to reject modern naturalism's excessive scientism, which we can do without violence to any genuine achievements of modern science.

I think that the whole issue of "modern naturalism" is a red herring. The need to populate the world with thinkable contents arises immediately from the demand that *the world* exercise *rational* control over our beliefs. But the deep source of McDowell's views is a conviction he shares with the philosophical tradition he is trying to escape: there is something to be said about "rational control" at the stratospheric level of "mind" and "world." McDowell's thought that "coherentism" is automatically "frictionless" is plausible only if coherentism is understood to imply radical holism. While I agree that this is the way coherentism should be understood, I want to insist on two things: that, by this criterion, contextualism is not coherentism, and that contextualism offers a way out of McDowell's dilemma that does not require us to re-enchant the world.

One reason for rejecting radically holistic coherentism is that this outlook encourages sceptically motivated questions like "What justifies the whole thing?" or "Why do belief-belief relations, which are wholly internal to belief-systems, make it likely that such systems are true of external reality?" These questions are all ways of voicing the suspicion that coherentism is frictionless: that it cuts thought loose from external constraint. However, the minimal "coherentism" of *Groundless Belief* is implicitly contextualist precisely because it is sceptical of "our beliefs" as a theoretically integrated totality about which justificational questions can usefully be raised. There are, I argue, only two ways to make the question "What justifies the whole thing?", or "How is 'mind' answerable to 'world'"? seem both dangerous and compelling. Either we are asking how "thought" relates to the world as an ineffable thing-in-itself, or we are wondering how the totality of our objective knowledge is constrained by the deliverances of experience. In the one case, we are misled by a hopelessly confused metaphor and, in the other, we assume the foundationalist picture of knowledge from the outset. The argument of *Groundless Belief* dissolves the problem to which McDowell's invitation to see the world itself as conceptually structured is a solution.

On the view I defend, the world contributes to the contexts in which doxastic revision is conducted by its causal influence on our observational beliefs. McDowell will reply that, if the world's influence on our beliefs is merely causal, our interactions with the world have nothing to do with justification. If (confusedly) we suppose that they do, we have regressed to the Myth of the Given. This is where he reads too much into "the unboundedness of the conceptual." To say that appropriate causation is never sufficient for knowledge is not the same as saying that causation is irrelevant to epistemic status: recall here my earlier discussion of the two aspects of justification, epistemic responsibility and grounding.

McDowell's plausible-sounding claim that causes can sometimes exculpate but can never justify falls apart in light of this distinction. If causes can exculpate, they are certainly relevant to epistemic responsibility, even though they are not evidence. And if grounding can be partially externalist, causes can be relevant to grounding, again without being evidence. The point of recognising a default and challenge structure in contextual justification is to allow that a person can have a justified belief—both in that he holds it in an epistemically responsible way and in that the belief itself is adequately grounded—without his holding it on the basis of evidence.

I have claimed that McDowell remains under the spell of the question "What justifies empirical knowledge as a whole?" I have also claimed that there are only two ways to understand this question: in terms of either foundationalism or radically holistic coherentism. If I am right on both counts, we should expect McDowell's unequivocal rejection of both frictionless coherentism and the Myth of the Given to lead him to an attempt to rehabilitate foundationalism by detaching it from the Myth. This is what I believe his position amounts to. Thus, he writes:

When we trace justifications back, the last thing we come to is still a thinkable content; not something more ultimate than that, a bare pointing to a bit of the Given. . . . The thinkable contents that are ultimate in the order of justification are contents of experiences, and in enjoying an experience one is open to manifest facts. . . .[10]

This is foundationalism without the Given. The idea of "the order of justification" is the essential commitment of the foundational conception of knowledge. It is this idea, not the disenchantment of the world by modern science, that underwrites the sceptical problems that have haunted modern philosophy. Indeed, it is this conception of a context-independent order of reasons—"epistemological realism"—that elevates "our knowledge of the world" into an object of theoretical inquiry.[11]

McDowell rejects the standard dilemma between foundationalism and the coherence theory in favour of one between the Given and coherence because he denies that epistemological problems, particularly sceptical problems, go deep. For McDowell, the deep issue is the possibility of genuine thought. There is less to this than meets the eye. It is by way of being frictionless that coherentism threatens to destroy content; and the thought that coherentism is frictionless is just another way of saying that it invites unanswerable sceptical questions. More than this, it seems to me that McDowell pays for his comparative indifference to epistemological issues. He may escape the choice between coherentism and the appeal to the Given. But because he remains committed to understanding the relation between "mind" and "world," the choice between foundationalism and the coherence theory continues to shape his thought.

What McDowell calls "empiricism" is what in *Groundless Belief* I call "phenomenalism." At the time, my motive for choosing this nonstandard terminology was my hope that empiricism might be detached from foundationalism. In particular, I wanted

[10] Ibid., p. 29
[11] See *Unnatural Doubts*, ch. 3.

to detach the idea that non-inferential observational knowledge plays an important role in justification from the foundationalist account of that role. Perhaps this is a vain hope. But if empiricism is wedded to foundationalism, so much the worse for empiricism.

5. The Death of Epistemology

Groundless Belief announces the death of epistemology, though not in a wholly unequivocal way. For while I say that we should move beyond epistemology, conceived as the discipline that places knowledge on its proper foundations, I also claim that the foundational picture's grip on our philosophical imagination can be broken only by an alternative picture. Still, I do not want to make too much of this, since I frequently hint that a non-foundational picture will be too trivial to be thought of as an epistemological theory. It is reasonable to take this to mean that epistemology as a serious theoretical enterprise is dead after all.

Whatever my uncertainties, others have presented a starker view. W. V. Quine and Richard Rorty claim without equivocation that traditional epistemology is dead.[12] And they do so on the basis of the equation I happily accept in the main text: epistemology aims at defending empirical knowledge by placing it on its proper foundations. True, where Quine thinks that epistemology can go on in a "naturalised" form as empirical psychology, Rorty thinks that this modest, empirical enterprise has too little in common with the grand enterprise of epistemology to be thought of as epistemology's continuation. But with respect to the prospects of epistemology as traditionally conceived, they have no serious disagreement.

I now think that the claim that epistemology should be either naturalised or eliminated reflects several questionable ideas,

[12] W. V. Quine, "Epistemology Naturalised" in *Ontological Relativity and Other Essays* (New York and London: Columbia University Press 1969). Richard Rorty, *Philosophy and the Mirror of Nature* (Princeton NJ: Princeton University Press 1979).

some of which are present in or implied by positions taken in *Groundless Belief.*

The first of these is an over-simplified identification of the goal of epistemology with "refuting the sceptic." This identification is not gratuitous: as I say, it is plausible on both historical and theoretical grounds. However, although I continue to think that coming to terms with scepticism has often been philosophical epistemology's central task, it has never been the sole motive for epistemological reflection. Other epistemological questions include:

> *Demarcation Problems.* Can we determine in a principled way what sorts of things we might reasonably expect to know about? Or, as is sometimes said, what are the scope and limits of human knowledge? Do some subjects lie within the province of knowledge while others are fated to remain in the province of opinion (or faith)? Do some apparently significant forms of discourse lie outside the realm of the "factual" or "meaningful" altogether?
>
> *Methodological Problems.* These include problems about how knowledge is to be obtained. Is there just one way of acquiring knowledge, or are there several, depending on the sort of knowledge in question? (For example, are there fundamental differences between the natural and the social or "human" sciences?) Can we improve our ways of seeking knowledge?
>
> *The Problem of Reason.* Are there methods of inquiry, or of fixing belief, that are distinctively rational? And, if so, what are they?

One reason scepticism has been taken so seriously is that it interacts in significant ways with concerns like these.

All of the above problems raise normative questions. This is to be expected. Epistemological terms are themselves normative. In trying to achieve a reflective understanding of epistemic evaluation, we are naturally guided by intuitive judgments about good epistemic practice. But making epistemic norms explicit can hardly fail to have normative implications. Epistemology is thus not just about normative practices: it is itself a normative undertaking. This is the main reason it cannot be "naturalised" in the sense of its being replaced by a wholly descriptive form of inquiry.

Quine and Rorty both reject the idea of normative epistemology. They do so because they equate this with the idea of epistemology as "first philosophy": an *a priori* discipline that stands outside science and judges it (Quine) or outside all other forms of discourse and judges them (Rorty). What is not so obvious, however, is that all epistemological concerns stand or fall with the project of judging our knowledge from what Quine calls a position of "cosmic exile," which in practice means responding to the sceptic by placing knowledge on suitably solid foundations. Why can't they arise, so to speak, from the inside, in response to changes in our ways of looking at the world?

Now, it is certainly possible to see responding to scepticism by way of some foundational project as the key to demarcational and methodological problems. For example, if we meet scepticism with empiricist foundationalism, we are likely to find that not all forms of discourse can easily be accommodated to the epistemic ideal, in which case we may feel compelled to dismiss them as "non-cognitive." Nevertheless, it would take a lot of argument to show that this is the only way to approach demarcational or methodological concerns.

A second questionable idea is the equation of "refuting the sceptic" with providing a *direct* response to sceptical arguments. I continue to think that this approach to scepticism leads in the end to some version of foundationalism. But there are indirect or diagnostic ways of responding to scepticism that have epistemological lessons to teach.

I am less than clear about this in the main text because I fail to distinguish between what I now call "therapeutic" and "theoretical" diagnoses.[13] A therapeutic diagnosis treats philosophical problems—epistemological problems included—as pseudo-problems generated by misuses or misunderstandings of lan-

---

[13] For more on this distinction, see *Unnatural Doubts*, ch. 1.

guage. By contrast, a theoretical diagnosis treats them as genuine, but only given a definite background of theoretical presuppositions. *Groundless Belief*, which traces a whole array of philosophical problems and doctrines to the foundational conception of knowledge, is an exercise in theoretical diagnosis.

To see the relevance of this distinction to the death of epistemology, note that a philosopher intent on killing epistemology off will neither claim to have solved epistemology's problems in a theoretical way nor admit that they are insoluble. Rather, his aim will be to eliminate (McDowell says "exorcise") all epistemological problems, obviating the need for theory. This task commits him to a therapeutic approach. If the problems were never genuine, they can be dissolved without leaving *any* theoretical residue.

Theoretical diagnosis does not encourage such ambitions. Because it works by identifying and criticising the assumptions hidden in traditional sceptical arguments, it inevitably suggests an alternative picture of knowledge. In *Groundless Belief*, I concede the need for such a picture but, under the spell of the therapeutic approach, imply that it will be free of all theoretical commitments and thus problem-free.

There is no reason to suppose that such a picture exists.

Index of Names